P R A I S E   F O R
Rise to Your Destiny,
Woman of God!

If you are a woman who has longed to break out of the limitations
keeping you back from your destiny in God, this book will be an encouragement to you. As Barbara deals with key issues such as our identity as
women, our role in leadership both in the Church and the workplace,
and the importance of mentoring, she raises a clarion call for us
to rise up and be all God intended us to be.

Jane Hansen
President and CEO, Aglow International

Rise to Your Destiny, Woman of God! That is more than a title—it is a
prophetic statement of God for this moment of the Church. And who better
to declare it than one of God's leading ladies, Barbara Wentroble! She is a
strong and mature woman carrying love and revelation for men as well as
women. Barbara does not come from a feminist or negative view in this book,
but declares a positive prophetic response. You need to read this book!

John P. Kelly
President, LEAD (Leadership Education for Apostolic Development)

Rise to Your Destiny, Woman of God is another great book Barbara has written
that needs to be in the hands of every woman. In the pages of this book,
Barbara encourages and compels us to start moving toward our full potential
and explains the way to get there. Barbara Wentroble lives this book.

Barbara J. Yoder
Senior Pastor, Shekinah Christian Church, Ann Arbor, MI
National Apostolic Council, United States Strategic Prayer Network

Barbara Wentroble not only writes clearly, concisely and profoundly
about God's call for women to rise up, alongside of men, in leadership on
all levels of church life, but she also models it in her own life and ministry.
Barbara's experience and practical insights as an apostle shine
through on every page of this groundbreaking book!

C. Peter Wagner
Chancellor, Wagner Leadership Institute

RISE *to* YOUR DESTINY WOMAN *of* GOD

Barbara Wentroble

Regal

From Gospel Light
Ventura, California, U.S.A.

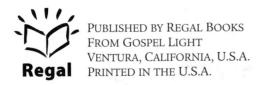

PUBLISHED BY REGAL BOOKS
FROM GOSPEL LIGHT
VENTURA, CALIFORNIA, U.S.A.
PRINTED IN THE U.S.A.

Regal Books is a ministry of Gospel Light, a Christian publisher dedicated to serving the local church. We believe God's vision for Gospel Light is to provide church leaders with biblical, user-friendly materials that will help them evangelize, disciple and minister to children, youth and families.

It is our prayer that this Regal book will help you discover biblical truth for your own life and help you meet the needs of others. May God richly bless you.

For a free catalog of resources from Regal Books/Gospel Light, please call your Christian supplier or contact us at 1-800-4-GOSPEL or www.regalbooks.com.

Library of Congress Cataloging-in-Publication Data
Wentroble, Barbara, 1943-
   Rise to your destiny, woman of God / Barbara Wentroble.
      p. cm.
   ISBN 0-8307-3903-3 (trade paper)
   1. Christian women—Religious life. 2. Self-realization in women. I. Title.
BV4527.W439 2006
248.8'43—dc22   2006009639

1   2   3   4   5   6   7   8   9   10   /   10   09   08   07   06

Rights for publishing this book in other languages are contracted by Gospel Light Worldwide, the international nonprofit ministry of Gospel Light. Gospel Light Worldwide also provides publishing and technical assistance to international publishers dedicated to producing Sunday School and Vacation Bible School curricula and books in the languages of the world. For additional information, visit www.gospellightworldwide.org; write to Gospel Light Worldwide, P.O. Box 3875, Ventura, CA 93006; or send an e-mail to info@gospellightworldwide.org.

Contents

Acknowledgments 7

Foreword. 9
J. Lee Grady

Chapter 1 13
Arise, Woman of God

Chapter 2 27
Changing Your Identity

Chapter 3 49
Dealing with Fears and Hindrances

Chapter 4 63
Partnership of Men and Women

Chapter 5 75
Women in Leadership

Chapter 6 87
Women in the Workplace

Chapter 7 99
Finding Mentors

Chapter 8 113
Chosen for Greatness

Conclusion. 123
A Hope and a Future

To six wonderful gifts the Lord has given me—
my granddaughters!

Anna

Annaliese

Gabriella

Kailee

Lindsey

Sylvia

As young apostolic women, may you arise and fulfill
God's destiny for your lives!

I once read that successful people never reach their goals alone. I heartily agree with that statement. Writing this book would have been impossible for me to do alone. In the midst of an extremely busy schedule, the Lord brought a number of gifted, anointed individuals to help me achieve my goal. I want to acknowledge several people who made this book possible.

How can I ever find the words to thank Norma Anderson? She spent innumerable hours researching, editing, advising and overseeing the entire writing of the manuscript. Her knowledge and sensitivity is truly a gift from God in my life!

I also want to thank my family. My husband, Dale, and my children, Brian, Lori and Mark are such an encouragement in my life. They constantly help to propel me into my destiny.

My daughters-in-law Michelle and Britt are like my own daughters. Thank you for your love and encouragement. My son-in-law Brian Kooiman always helps me find the peaceful place in the midst of a busy lifestyle.

My staff at International Breakthrough Ministries (IbM) went the extra mile and miles to help me achieve my vision. They always make me look good!

The intercessors led by Falma Rufus prayed me into each new level and covered this book with powerful intercession.

The IbM Apostolic Network linked arms with me to write a book that will affect the nations of the world.

Steven Lawson, Kim Bangs, Bill Greig III and the entire staff at Gospel Light worked hard to see this project completed. Cathi Macias did a terrific job on the final editing. What a blessing it is to work with you!

I also want to thank the Lord Jesus Christ. Without You I can do nothing! You made all this possible. May this book bring glory and honor to Your Name!

We don't hear many sermons today about the women who served on the apostle Paul's ministry team. Of course, the men who worked alongside Paul are often applauded. We often hear about Timothy, Paul's beloved son in the faith, and we often read about Titus and Barnabas.

Yet in all my years growing up in a traditional church, I have never heard a pastor speak about Phoebe (who is called a "deacon" in Romans 16:1-2), Euodia and Syntyche (who were full-time women ministers mentioned in Philippians 4:2-3), or Philip's four daughters (who were prophets, mentioned in Acts 21:9). And I certainly never heard a sermon about the woman named Junia, who served with Paul as a respected apostle (see Romans 16:7). Junia had the honor of going to prison for her faith, yet most Christians have never heard of her.

Even in contemporary charismatic churches that claim to have special revelation about the Holy Spirit, we rarely hear leaders preach about these powerful women of God who helped turn the world upside down during the first century. Why don't leaders talk about these women? Why do we ignore them? It is because the concept of women in fivefold ministry does not fit into our narrow religious paradigms. For years, conservative Christians who claim to believe the entire Bible have negated huge portions of God's Word because of wrong mind-sets about women in ministry.

The truth is set forth clearly in the New Testament. When the Holy Spirit was poured out on the first disciples, many of Jesus' women followers were there. They heard the sound of the mighty rushing wind. They saw tongues of fire descending from heaven on each believer. They spoke in tongues, just as the men did. When the apostle Peter preached on the Day of Pentecost and quoted Joel 2:28, those women claimed the promise for themselves: "In the last days . . . I will pour out My Spirit on all people. Your sons and *daughters* will prophesy" (Acts 2:17, *NIV*, emphasis added).

Since the church began, Jesus Christ has always reserved a portion for His daughters. He did not ignore them. He commissioned His female followers to receive His power, preach the gospel, heal the sick, cast out devils and claim nations for His kingdom. And the women of the New Testament took Him seriously.

Because of male pride, chauvinism and religious prejudice, many in the Church have ignored the key role that women are destined to play in the work of the ministry. Many have distorted the true message of the Bible and misinterpreted certain difficult passages in Paul's writings, creating doctrines and policies that restrict women rather than releasing and empowering them. But I am thankful that in this special hour of global revival God is restoring to us the truth that says women are indeed called to serve alongside men as coequal partners in the gospel.

This concept of equality in ministry is beautifully demonstrated in the life of Priscilla, a powerful Bible teacher and apostolic woman who worked with Paul (see Acts 18:24-26). Although she was married to Aquilla, the Bible does not suggest that she played a subordinate role in ministry. In fact, in three of the six times she is mentioned in the Bible, her name is listed before her husband's. Scholars believe that is because this godly Roman woman was regarded as an authority in the Church.

Why don't we hear sermons about Priscilla's ministry? After all, she was a true mother in the faith. She and her husband traveled with Paul and often stayed behind after he left in order to strengthen the new churches that had been planted in Asia Minor and Europe. Priscilla knew the Word of God. She brought churches into apostolic order. She even helped instruct the man named Apollos—and launched him into apostolic ministry. She is a model for our times—because in this day of spiritual compromise and weak-kneed church leadership, we need apostolic women to arise and take their place in the Church.

When I read about Priscilla, I often think of my friend Barbara Wentroble. Since 2005, I have had the opportunity to preach with Barbara in special conferences designed to train women for ministry. Barbara is a modern example of an apostolic woman. She knows the Word of God and does not compromise it. She prays with authority, preaches with power and calls Christians to radical commitment.

Even though she is not old enough to be my mother, I consider her a mother in the faith. I value her personal counsel and hang on every word she speaks from the pulpit. I am cheering her on, and I am praying that through her influence, many women around the world will discover that their spiritual destiny is not limited to being a wife, a mother or a nursery worker—even though those roles are important. Barbara is a wife, a mother and a grandmother, too—but she knows that women can also change nations and trample on the devil's works.

This book is going to ignite a holy passion in a new generation of Priscillas, Phoebes and Junias. I pray that every woman who reads this book will arise, take up her spiritual weapons and plunder the enemy.

J. Lee Grady
Editor, *Charisma*
Author, *Ten Lies the Church Tells Women*

Arise, Woman of God

As I watched the 2006 Winter Olympics, I was amazed (as I always am) at the grace and strength exhibited by the participants. Whether swooshing down a snow-covered mountainside or gliding across the ice on blades of steel, it is obvious that these athletes' magnificent feats are preceded by countless hours of dedication and discipline.

Something even more amazing to me, however, is watching the Special Olympics. Although these participants may not appear as graceful or refined as their Olympic counterparts, their determination and discipline to break out of the limitations of their physical or mental disabilities is even more evident and heartwarming. I find myself both challenged and inspired as I watch these valiant athletes perform to their utmost, for I know they have overcome great obstacles—and many naysayers— to get there.

I thought of those Special Olympians one day as I observed my two young granddaughters, Lindsey and Kailee, who were spending the evening at my home. They had pulled out a coloring book and crayons and were trying to outdo each other as they colored all over the pages. Rather than correct them by saying,

"Slow down, girls, and stay inside the lines," I decided instead to encourage them to break out of their natural limitations. "That's the way to do it!" I said. "Get outside those lines! Make your own designs. Don't get boxed in by someone else's idea of what the picture should look like."

Although encouraging children to color outside of the lines to create their own designs may seem inconsequential, it can be a step in the right direction of fulfilling God's purpose for their lives. If someone hadn't encouraged those Special Olympics participants to "color outside the lines," they might never have realized how big they could dream or how far they could go.

Today, God is calling women to color outside the lines—to arise and break out of the limitations that life, religion and tradition have placed on them. Many women are answering, but many are still tied to traditions and regulations that prevent them from experiencing the joy that comes from walking in the steps God has ordered for them.

How well I can relate! As a child, limitations were normal for me. I grew up in a home in which the maxim of children being seen and not heard was the order of the day. Even when I did not actually hear those words being spoken, the atmosphere was filled with the meaning. By the time I reached adulthood, I had learned to live in an environment in which I suppressed my feelings, opinions and way of vocalizing my thoughts. Because my words were restricted, I grew up believing that they were not important, and I soon developed a fear of speaking. I learned to live in a manner devoid of personal expression, feeling that I had nothing of value to offer.

Church life didn't seem to be much different from what I experienced at home. As a child, I went to church every Sunday. My parents did not attend, but they always made sure that we children did. Through all those years of listening to church sermons and Sunday School lessons, as well as seeing many of those sermons and lessons modeled by church leadership, I quickly surmised that there were limitations on what women could do in church. The following are some of those limitations:

- Women are to keep silent in the church (much like my home life in which children were not to be heard!).
- Women can only teach boys until they reach the age of 12. After that, women can teach only girls and other women.
- Women can sing in the choir and occasionally lead worship, but they can never preach from the pulpit.
- Women can preach if they go to the jungles of Africa or some other country as a missionary, but they simply cannot preach in the pulpits of churches in the United States.
- Women cannot pastor a church or serve in church government positions (such as a deacon or elder).
- Women must always submit to men—and submission means blind obedience.

Although I accepted these teachings and limitations, there burned within me such a desire to break out of those boundaries that the situation became a great source of inner conflict and turmoil. How could I live out the desires within my heart and yet obey God at the same time? I loved God and wanted to obey Him, so if pleasing the Lord meant living within the barriers that I learned in my home and in my church, I would need to accept my lot in life. It seemed that I had no choice, and so I resigned myself to walk within the lines.

Sadly, I did not realize that by doing so I had aligned myself with the enemy of my soul, signing an unwritten contract that would prevent me from fulfilling my God-given destiny. Although I thought that I had submitted myself to God, I had instead locked myself into boundaries that God had never intended for me.

Through the years, I have talked with many women who have signed the same unwritten contract and have accepted the same unintended boundaries. They struggle with inner dreams, visions and desires. They love God with their whole heart and want to obey Him, but limitations have been put on them that restrict them from ever being able to live out those dreams and desires.

Lines are limitations that define the borders and restrictions in our lives. Of course, not all limitations are bad. Without certain limitations in society, we would have anarchy. Speed limits, laws against crime or murder, and even building codes are designed to help people live in a safe environment. But the limitations we're discussing here go far beyond sensible and necessary protections for our well-being.

A few years ago, I attended a meeting with about 400 women leaders from several nations. One prominent woman, a speaker and author named Linda, candidly shared her testimony with us. She told us that she grew up in a home that was not Christian. Throughout her childhood, Linda's mother told her that she could do anything if she would just be strong and continue to press forward. This was the positive and encouraging message that Linda continually heard as she grew up in her non-Christian home.

After she was born again, Linda started attending church as an adult. She was shocked when, for the first time in her life, she was told that there were some things that she *could not do* in church. She could not preach. She could not teach men. She could not be in church government. The reason she could not do these things was not because she was not smart enough, educated enough or qualified enough. She could not do them simply because she was a woman.

Linda is not the only woman who has experienced these limitations in her life. Maybe you have heard some of the same things spoken into your own life. If so, I have good news for you. Jesus came to set the captives free (see Luke 4:18). The Spirit of Truth has come to reveal the heart

> *God* has a plan for you and, according to Scriptures, it's a good plan: to give you a future and a hope.

of the Father concerning God's plan for women (see John 15:26). He has a plan for you and, according to the Scriptures, it is a good plan: to give you a future and a hope.

> "For I know the plans that I have for you," declares the LORD, "plans for welfare and not for calamity to give you a future and a hope" (Jer. 29:11).

You were born for this hour in history because God Himself ordained it so. He has a wonderful destiny set aside with your name on it!

Anne Graham Lotz, founder and president of AnGel Ministries, is coloring outside the lines in her own life and ministry. For more than 30 years, she has proclaimed the Word of God to people all around the world. In 2000, she began the Just Give Me Jesus events as a time of "refreshing for women" in cities across the nation (events have been held in the Ukraine, South Korea, England, Wales, Puerto Rico, Paraguay and Panama as well). Anne's father, evangelist Billy Graham, is supportive of Anne's desire to color outside the lines, as so many others have done.

Rachel Saint is a perfect example of a woman who refused to be confined to someone else's boundaries. When Rachel's husband, Nate, and four other missionaries were killed by the fierce Waodani tribe in the eastern rainforests of Ecuador in the 1950s, Rachel decided to purposely step outside the lines. With the other family members of the slain missionaries, Rachel returned to the Waodanis and completed the work that her husband and the others had started. She and her companions brought the gospel of salvation to this isolated tribe (which was in danger of extinction due to its own barbaric behavior) and established the light of God's glory among a people who were once in darkness.

And then there is Condoleeza Rice who, prior to becoming Secretary of State, served as Assistant to the President for National Security Affairs in the United States (commonly referred to as the National Security Advisor). Dr. Rice is a wonderful role model not only for women but also for anyone who doesn't want to get boxed in by someone else's lines. Today, God is calling women to arise out of a limited revelation of God's plan for their lives and fulfill their purpose and destiny.

Several years ago, I had a profound vision. I was watching as a small wave washed up on the shore and then slowly receded. Wave after wave continued to come ashore, each a little higher than the previous one. Suddenly, the largest wave I have ever seen rolled into view. As I watched, it came onto the land and circled the globe, covering the nations.

"What am I seeing?" I asked the Lord. I sensed Him revealing to me that each small wave represented a move of His Holy Spirit, each carrying a measure of revelation that was higher than the previous move. He then revealed to me that a move of His Spirit was coming that would be greater than all previous moves of His Spirit.

The tsunami of December 2004 reminded me of that vision. Scientists tell us that a tsunami occurs when there is a shift in the plates of the earth. Changing electromagnetic fields affect gravity, and the shift causes an undersea earthquake, which results in a monstrous wave. Although my vision of the waves was given to me many years before the disastrous tsunami of 2004, that vision is as clear today as it was when I first received it. Prior to the 2004 tsunami, a shift took place in the plates of the earth. That natural shift is symbolic of a spiritual shift that is taking place right now as the Lord releases great revelation concerning His plans for women throughout the world.

Part of God's revelation involves the partnership of men and women to influence the nations of the world. God is calling women to arise and walk in equal partnership with men. God always planned for men and women to walk in convergence and fulfill His purpose in the earth. The Bible teaches that both men and women were created in God's image. Both had a direct relationship with God. Both shared the responsibilities of bearing and rearing children and having dominion over the created order (see Gen. 1:26-28). Jesus always taught that all believers, regardless of gender or race or social status, are necessary and beneficial to the Body of Christ.

At Pentecost, the Holy Spirit came upon men and women alike. Both were given gifts without discrimination or preference (see Acts 2:1-21; 1 Cor. 12:7,11; 14:31). Men and women are called by the Lord to develop and exercise those gifts as good stewards of the grace of God. Yet, although this partnership is the will of God, His will does not always get done on Earth as it does in heaven. In fact, some respected theologians and reformers throughout history have taught contrary to these principles.

In *10 Lies the Church Tells Women*, J. Lee Grady quotes Tertullian, a respected Church father who lived during the second century. Tertullian blamed the world's problems on women. His opinions were accepted by many of the earliest Christians. He said:

> You [women] are the devil's gateway; you are the unsealer of that [forbidden] tree; you are the first deserter of the divine law; you are she who persecuted him whom the devil was not vigilant enough to attack. You destroyed so easily God's image, man. On account of your desert [punishment]—that is, death—even the Son of God had to die.[1]

Not only did some theologians teach this faulty doctrine, but many of the "reformers" also continued to propagate it. Men such as Martin Luther and John Calvin failed to understand God's complete role for women. They saw women only in a domestic role. Women, from the view of Luther and Calvin and others like them, were on the earth to serve in the home, have sex with their husbands, and bear children. How sad that the oppression of women has not only been tolerated in the Church but has also been taught as the will of God!

Jesus came to redeem *all* people—women as well as men: "For God so loved the world [all men and women] that He gave His only begotten Son, that whoever believes in Him should not perish but have everlasting life" (John 3:16, *NKJV*). Through faith in Christ, we all become children of God. We are one in Christ, and we all share as heirs of the blessings of salvation. In Christ, there are no distinctions with regard to racial, social or gender bias (see John 1:12-13; Rom. 8:14-17; 2 Cor. 5:17; Gal. 3:26-28).

Walls of division between men and women are crumbling. During the 1980s, the walls of Eastern Europe began to fall. Nation after nation completely changed as those walls came down. Those nations in the Eastern Bloc had been confined and restricted by certain mind-sets, or "boxes," and the people living there did not have freedom. Suddenly, they were set free from the confines of those boxes. Now, they are free from the communist stronghold and are in productive partnerships with many other nations in the world.

> *God* is empowering a new generation of men and women to walk side by side and press into every area of life with great victory.

Today, the walls that have kept men and women from walking together in full partnership are crumbling and falling as surely as the wall that once separated Eastern and Western Europe. Jesus came to tear down *every* dividing wall and to set people free to serve Him and to minister in His name. "For He Himself is our peace, who made both groups into one, and broke down the barrier of the dividing wall" (Eph. 2:14).

Oppression and cruelty toward women is also crumbling. God is empowering a new generation of men and women to walk side by side and press into every area of life with great victory. A shift has taken place in the earth. A tsunami of God's Spirit is crumbling every wall that keeps men and women from fulfilling His purpose. Together, men and women are arising in partnership to bring transformation to the nations of the earth!

God is calling out to women today to arise. Arise out of your captivity! Arise out of religious restrictions! Arise out of traditional mind-sets that are contrary to the will of God for your life! Arise with a new freedom that allows you to explore God's plan for you, in a similar way that explorers search out new territory.

Let me give you an example from my own life, as recorded in my book *God's Purpose for Your Life*:

> While vacationing in the Canadian Rockies, we visited the Colombian Icefield and the Athabasca Glacier. As I viewed the history in the visitor's center, my eyes were drawn to a plaque that described a couple of the pioneers who explored the area. Wooley and Collie were men who dared to brave the severe weather and hazards of the icefield. Unlike the negative responses of other explorers of the area, these men saw something positive. Rather than seeing the difficulties of the terrain, they saw an incredible challenge ahead to discover that which had been hidden from previous generations. The plaque bearing their names has this inscription:
>
>> Wooley and Collie—It fell to two other explorers, Herman Wooley and J. Norman Collie, to finally realize the magnitude of what lay before them. The year was 1898 when Collie gave this breathless description of the Columbia Icefield: "A new world was spread at our feet: to the west stretched a vast icefield probably never before seen by human eye, and surrounded by entirely unknown, unnamed and unclimbed peaks." The mountains were no longer fearful, now they had become a challenge to be conquered.

Wooley and Collie were men who were willing to climb to great heights to pave a way for others. They were willing to explore the unknown. They sacrificed the comforts of life and risked their own lives for future generations. They climbed great heights to see the previously unseen. As mighty men, they were like great "eagles" in history.[2]

Today, I feel like an eagle. I am living outside the religious limitations that I experienced when I was growing up. The Lord allows me to minister alongside men throughout many nations of the world. I am part of the leadership team for my church. I also oversee a network of churches and leaders, made up of both men and women.

None of this happened overnight. I first had to go through a long process of what the Bible refers to as "renewing my mind" (see Rom. 12:2), which included meditating on God's Word, spending extensive time in prayer, receiving by faith prophecies that were spoken over me, and dying to my own feelings and thoughts so that I might walk according to God's purposes and not my own.

God had a plan for my life, but I had to arise out of the religious thinking that I learned while I was growing up. You may not be called to do exactly what I am doing, but you are called to do what the Lord has created you to do. Religious thinking can keep you from leading your children in the right direction, being a leader of the PTA, or accepting a position at work. It is time for you to arise and break out of old religious mind-sets that have kept you from fulfilling your destiny.

As women, we must not live merely for ourselves. We must arise and break free for future generations. God wants to help us be a part of painting a new picture of life for His women. He wants all His people to color outside of the restrictive lines that others have used to quash our creativity and damage our destiny. We must do this so that our children and grandchildren can also apprehend God's plan for their lives.

Like Queen Esther, you were born for such a time as this (see Esther 4:14). Your family, the Body of Christ, the Lord Himself, and even society need you to be free. In Matthew 21:2-3, Jesus told His disciples, "Go into the village opposite you, and immediately you will find a donkey tied there and a colt with her; untie them and bring them to Me. If anyone says anything to you, you shall say, 'The Lord has need of them.'" As women, we are being set free in the same way.

Do not allow your age, your culture, your educational background, your religion, your finances, your traditions or your fears to keep you from your finest moment. Your time from the Lord has arrived. So, woman of God, arise to your God-given destiny and become who you really are!

And who is that? Who are you, *really*? For the question is not who you *think* you are, but who you *really* are. Your identity may need to change in order for you to fulfill your destiny. In the next chapter, we'll take a look at what is involved for you to arise and become the *real you* that God created you to be.

Discussion Questions

1. List some of the phrases or expressions you heard growing up that helped frame your thinking. How did they affect your developing personality?

2. What were some of the good limitations that you received during your early years?

3. Describe your previous understanding of your role as a Christian woman.

4. How do you function or fail to function in partnership with men?

5. Describe the way you are overcoming old religious mind-sets concerning women.

6. Describe some practical ways you are allowing the *real you* to come forth in your life.

Notes
1. J. Lee Grady, *10 Lies the Church Tells Women* (Lake Mary, FL: Creation House, 2000), p. 21.
2. Barbara Wentroble, *God's Purpose for Your Life* (Ventura, CA: Regal Books, 2002), p. 184.

Changing Your Identity

"Identity theft is the fastest-growing crime in the United States." When I heard the TV newscaster's words, I was shocked. It wasn't so much that I wasn't aware of the problem of identity theft—but the fastest-growing crime in the United States? I would have thought that it would have been violent crimes, murders or drug offenses, with identity theft somewhere near the bottom of the list.

I thought about that report for several days. Although I knew the program was reporting on a problem in the natural realm, I sensed the Lord revealing a spiritual problem in the Body of Christ: Women throughout history have suffered from identity theft. Candi, whose story follows, is a classic example:

I had been rejected and physically, emotionally and psychologically abused as a child primarily by a family member right on up through my teen years. This person would say things to me like, "You're never going to amount to anything" or "You're never going anywhere in life."

Right after graduating from high school, I started a job at a major corporation, and made a good salary. However, I didn't feel that this was good enough for me. I believed that I had to prove to my family and to the world that I was somebody—that I was significant.

Within a 20-year span of time, I worked myself into a highly paid middle-management position. Then, when the company decided to let people go, I volunteered so that I could get the severance package and go back to school for my Masters Degree.

My goals were to continue to climb the corporate ladder and to add to my identity as a powerful woman. I planned to work at the top executive level with the CEO and the management team. I soon received an offer from another blue-chip corporation, and my salary doubled to six figures.

I had achieved my ultimate dream—to be "somebody" and prove to others that I was worthy and significant. The company had high expectations and basically owned me. I spent anywhere from 60 to 80 hours per week working for the company.

Between my training and meeting corporate demands, I began to realize that I had achieved my ultimate goal. Unfortunately, I also realized that I was miserable. I had all kinds of feelings of anger and fear about what I had done to achieve my accomplishments, but I had no idea how to reverse or fix the problem.

I had a young family at home that I had been neglecting, along with everything else in life, while I pursued my goals and dreams. Then one day, after a year and a half of working and completing my Masters Degree, I felt the

Lord giving me great grace and peace to make a decision to resign and stay at home. I had no idea at the time what this would mean to me or anyone else. But I finally did it. I quit my "dream job" and went home to take care of my family.

Talk about an identity crisis! Who was I now? I knew I was a mother and wife, but what did that mean? What was I supposed to *do*?

Before I left my job, many of my business associates tried to talk me out of my decision. They said things like, "Are you crazy? Why would you leave everything you have worked so hard to achieve to stay home with your family?" Before long, I began to wonder the same thing. What had I done?

I continued to struggle with my identity for several years after leaving corporate America. Up to that point, I had found all my worth in the positions of power and titles that I held. I was scared to death about being home with a family. I hadn't realized that I had been running from my family, and I didn't know how to be a mother and wife. I was also well aware of how people in corporate settings viewed people who stayed home. I suddenly felt like a woman without a country. My family members, however, asked why I hadn't done this sooner.

During that transition time, God strategically placed me in churches that had teaching, healing, deliverance and restoration-of-family programs. I attended them faithfully, and God revealed Himself in powerful ways that demonstrated His love for me.

I began to work through much of the pain of my early years by getting back in touch with my parents. My mom and dad and I have reconciled and are now working together to break every bloodline curse. We are establishing God's covenant within our bloodline and for future generations. For my parents' fiftieth anniversary, we had blessing parties, during which my dad gave me his blessing as his firstborn daughter. When my children were 13 and 16, we also had blessing parties and made declarations over them.

God is healing and restoring my family. My son has been saved, baptized in the Holy Spirit, and water-baptized. My prodigal daughter is in her turnaround back to the Lord. And I know my husband's salvation is near. But the first step of this healing journey was for me to begin to realize my true identity in Christ.

Candi's story is one of many I've heard over the years, in addition to my own. I was no different from so many other women in that I grew up not knowing who I was. Oh, I knew who my parents were, of course. (Tragically, some women don't even know that.) I knew I was female. I knew my name was Barbara. I knew I was American. But my true identity seemed to be a mystery.

When asked, I described myself by the symptoms in my life. For instance, I would say:

- I am fearful.
- I am timid.
- I am insecure.
- I am shy.
- I am bashful.

I thought those words defined me, and I lived my life out of that understanding. I did not realize that life could be any different for me. After all, I had never known anything else. As strange as it may sound, I failed to understand that I was only existing and not really living.

My lack of understanding of my identity was especially difficult during my school years. When the teachers would ask the class a question, I was too timid and insecure to raise my hand, even though I usually knew the answer. I was just too afraid to take a chance and answer in front of my classmates. What if I gave the wrong answer? I couldn't stand the thought of having people, particularly my peers, laugh at me.

Then there were the dreams. Frequently, I dreamed of standing at a bus stop. As the bus approached, I noticed that I did not have my clothes on. I would wake from the dream in fear and near panic at the thought of not being ready. Later in life I realized that those dreams were common to many people, but as a child, I was sure that I was the only one with such frightening experiences. I also realized, as an adult, that those frightening dreams were speaking to me of my insecurity and fears. The bus represented my ride in life, and I was unprepared for the journey because my identity was missing. I did not know who God made me to be because my true identity had been stolen, and that left me feeling fearful and anxious.

The loss of true identity is part of the enemy's plan to keep us from living life to its fullest.

How can we be expected to deal with life when we are disconnected from our identity? My dreams were speaking to me of this problem and also of my deep feelings connected to it. Sometimes, dreams are used by the Lord as part of His prophetic communication to His people. He desires to speak to us and reveal that He has a better plan for our lives, but first He must help us discover our true identity so that we can be free from the fear and negative thoughts and feelings that hold us back.

The loss of true identity is part of the enemy's plan to keep us from living life to its fullest. As we read in Proverbs 23:7, whatever we believe in our heart determines the way we live our lives: "For as he thinks within himself, so he is." Not knowing who we are is a terrible waste of the life that God has given us.

One of the saddest stories in the Bible of people who did not know their own identity is recorded in Numbers 13. Moses, in response to God's direction, appointed a group of men to go into the Promised Land ahead of the Israelites to check it out. Unfortunately, when the group returned, all but two of the men gave a negative report, which planted seeds of doubt and fear in the minds of the Israelites:

> The land through which we have gone as spies is a land that devours its inhabitants, and all the people whom we saw in it are men of great stature. There we saw the giants (the descendants of Anak came from the giants); and *we were like grasshoppers in our own sight*, and so we were in their sight (vv. 32-33, *NKJV*, emphasis added).

Despite God's promise to give this land to the Israelites, these cowardly men reported that the inhabitants of the lands were "giants," while at the same time saying that they saw themselves "like grasshoppers." This has to be the worst case of mistaken identity that I've ever heard! These men, who represented the all-powerful God of the Israelites and who had witnessed that same God perform amazing miracles on their behalf, saw themselves as grasshoppers rather than victorious warriors. What a tragedy!

Thankfully, there were two men among them—Caleb and Joshua—whose identity had not been stolen. Look at their report, as compared to the negative report of those who saw themselves as grasshoppers:

> Let us go up at once and take possession, for *we are well able to overcome it* (v. 30, emphasis added).

Joshua and Caleb were not foolish enough to think that in their own strength they could storm the borders of the Promised Land and take it from its existing inhabitants. However, they knew who they were as representatives of the God of Israel, and that He would go ahead of them and clear the way.

That's where I am today. I recognize that I am a representative of the living God, as well as His child, and that His strength is my strength. I now know that the fears I had as a child were based on an incorrect assessment of my identity. I saw myself as a grasshopper rather than as a warrior and servant of God with unlimited potential. I can now say with confidence that I am an apostle, wearing a dual mantle that includes prophet. Why do I know and accept this? Because the Lord has revealed to me my true identity. He has shown me who I was created to be. The Lord first had to reveal to me my true identity before He could reveal what He wanted me to do.

The unveiling of this understanding of who I was in the Lord began during worship at a conference I was attending. As we sang a very simple song that I had learned as a child, "Jesus loves me, this I know, for the Bible tells me so," I suddenly had a vision. It was as if my eyes were opened, and I could see a little girl about four or five years old. She was dressed in a ruffled white dress and had a white bow in her hair. I watched as she ran toward Jesus, who was standing so tall and so strong in front of her. He bent down and scooped her up in His big, powerful arms, and held her close. Watching all this, I felt the fear, insecurity and timidity drain out of the little girl.

Although at that moment I did not understand what was happening, I knew that something had taken place in me. Later, I realized that the little girl was me. From that moment, healing occurred inside of me. My journey toward my new identity began. I was now on the path of discovering who I was in Jesus. I began to realize that because I was His child, I had no room for fear, timidity and insecurity. I could be safe and secure in Him.

God spoke not only to my heart about my identity in Him but also about what He has called me to do. The Lord has used credible prophets to speak to me through the years. My family and others who know me well have also affirmed me. The Lord has spoken through the gifts and anointings in my life as well as through the results of my ministry. Because I now know who I am, I also know what I have been called to do.

Recovery of our true identity occurs in many ways. The Lord may have people speak prophetic words into our lives. Various people may affirm who we are and what the Lord has called us to do. Sometimes, we may get a strong inner sense of God's identity for our lives. The fruit of our lives and work will also reveal who we really are. However, as Candi mentioned in her story, recovering our true identity is a process that will take time. Although we may begin the recovery process immediately, as happened to me when I had the vision of the little girl and Jesus, the entire understanding of our true identity will not happen in an instant. In my own life, I endured great struggles as I emerged into my true identity. Years passed as the Lord unveiled the mystery. He will do the same in your life.

It is no different in the natural world. When someone realizes that his or her identity has been stolen, that is only the beginning of a long and sometimes painful process of recovery. The person trying to recover his or her identity must call banks, creditors, credit reporting agencies and law enforcement officials. Even then, it can take years for that person to completely clear his or her record of bogus charges. However, as long as he or she is not dissuaded from the task at hand by difficult or uncooperative people or circumstances, the person's tenacity and determination to recover his or her identity will finally win out.

As Christian women, recognizing that our true identity is found only in our relationship with the very God of the Universe gives us the strength and determination to press on into a fulfillment of our destiny, which often includes the revelation of our uniqueness. Sometimes during that process, we find that we don't seem to be like the model of other women we see around us, and this can present difficulties. Candi felt the need to leave her corporate job and go home to care for her family, but many of her friends and coworkers thought she was crazy to even consider it.

In my case, I tried for years to fit into the "acceptable" women's meetings, meaning that I tried to look nice, smell nice and say nice things. But even though I was able to fit in because of my extreme efforts to do so, it was as if there were a raging lion inside me seeking to be released. I hated attending those meetings. They seemed so mindless and inconsequential.

The meetings I attended often included fashion shows, which were definitely not something I enjoyed, as I usually buy several mix-and-match outfits and wear them for years—not to mention the fact that the models usually wore clothes that I would never dream of wearing. They also included the occasional exchange of recipes. When my children were growing up, I cooked to keep them fed and healthy, not because I enjoyed cooking. (Today, due to my schedule and the fact that my children are no longer living at home, I seldom cook at all.) Once again, I just didn't fit in at these meetings.

Many of these meetings I attended also offered a door prize. Usually, these prizes were contributed by various businesses (I always thought they donated them because no one else wanted them). I wasn't in the least interested in any prizes or any doors, other than the door to heaven (see Rev. 4:1). Obviously, then, with my lack of concern for fashion, cooking or prizes, I had little incentive to attend these women's meetings. I just had to accept that I did not fit the profile and move on.

As we transition through the process of moving from the person we think we are to the person we really are, we sometimes may try to walk in our new identity before we are fully ready to do so. My young granddaughter Lindsey demonstrated that transitional dilemma when she was asked to be the flower girl in a wedding. Standing before the mirrors at the bridal shop, dressed in her long flower girl dress, she extended her hand toward her mother and commanded, "Say, 'Your Majesty.'" Lindsey wanted those watching her to realize that she was not merely a five-year-old; she was clothed as an important part of the wedding party. She did not want people addressing her by her familiar name, but rather she wanted to be identified as "Your Majesty." Her identity needed to change for this new phase in her life, so she was struggling to be sure that those around her noticed the change.

Others react differently, refusing to accept the change of identity and the resulting change of responsibilities that go with it. Julie, a first-grade teacher, remembers one particular year when school had just resumed after summer vacation. A little girl with blond braids bounced into class in the morning, eyes shining with anticipation of her new identity as a first-grader. She got through the morning just fine, but when the bell rang at noon and everyone lined up to go to the cafeteria for lunch, the little girl picked up her backpack and headed for the back door.

"Where are you going?" Julie asked.

"Home," the little girl replied.

Julie smiled and walked over to her. "Honey, when you were a kindergartner, you went home when the bell rang at noon. But now that you're a first-grader, you don't go home at noon anymore. The first-graders go to the cafeteria for lunch, and then they come back here to the classroom for the rest of the afternoon."

> *It* is often easier for us to simply remain trapped in misguided teachings and outdated traditions than to step outside of the deceptive safety of our restrictive but familiar lines.

As realization dawned on the little girl's face, she dropped her backpack to the floor, put her hands on her hips, and squinted her eyes at Julie. "Well, who signed me up for that?" she asked.

We laugh at the little girl's naiveté and immaturity, but don't we all behave just like her at times? I can't tell you how often as I grew in my true identity in Christ that I wanted to stop, put my hands on my hips, and demand, "Well, who signed me up for that?"

You see, it is sometimes easier for us *not* to discover our true identity or fulfill our God-given destiny. It is often easier for us to simply remain trapped in misguided teachings and outdated traditions than to keep putting one foot in front of the other and step farther and farther outside the deceptive safety of our restrictive but familiar lines. During the struggle, some people even try to disconnect from the people who previously have been a significant part of their lives.

A friend told me the story of her teenage son who tried to disconnect his identity from that of his family. He loved it when his mom dropped him off at school during his early school years, but after he reached the age of 13, things changed. Now, he wanted his mother to drop him off several blocks away from the school. He would rather walk a few blocks than have his friends see him arrive with his parents. After all, he was no longer a child. In fact, he probably thought he was an adult. The young teenager also didn't want to be seen in his mother's Cadillac. He wanted to be seen in a pickup truck. "Cadillacs are for women," he reasoned, "but pickup trucks are for men."

Although this teenage boy was no longer a child, neither was he an adult. His identity was changing, but he was not yet the man he would someday become. When we transition out of an old identity, we sometimes don't want others to identify us with people who have been in our lives in the past. We want to be known for the identity into which we are growing, rather than the identity we had when we were known solely for our connection with someone else.

This can also be true of an identity we once had that was connected to some act or function we performed in the past. For instance, if you once worked at a fast-food restaurant but now are progressing to a better job because of your education and/or training, you would probably prefer not to be identified by your past employment. I have watched many women in transition from an old identity. Some don't want people to think of them in connection to former relationships or circumstances. Some even strive to put distance between themselves and old friends for fear that someone will identify them in an old way.

Striving and fear are not from the Lord. It is God who will validate our identity, not us. Whatever we build, we will always need to maintain. If we are the one building our identity, we will always find ourselves struggling to prove it. But if the Lord brings us into a new identity, He will also reveal it to others. How wonderful when we can relax and enjoy what the Lord is doing in our life!

Part of the struggle we will face during the transition into our new identity may come from within our own household. Families don't always understand our change of identity. A woman who finds herself involved in ministry after being a mother and wife for many years, or a woman like Candi who leaves a successful career to care full-time for her family, typically experiences family-related difficulties. For instance, I remember when I first started speaking at meetings. Prior to that, I had always done the laundry, cooked the meals and cleaned the house. Suddenly, I was involved in ministry, and it was difficult to find the time to continue doing these same things at home.

I quickly learned to cook enough meals to last my family the entire time I was away. After preparing the meals and putting them in the freezer, I would put a schedule and heating instructions for the meals on the refrigerator. On many occasions, I would return home from the trip to find the meals untouched in the freezer. When I asked why they had not been eaten, the standard reply was always, "We decided we wanted to order pizza."

It took some time for me to realize that I was called to do more than cook meals and do laundry. Of course, not every woman is called to leave home and become involved in public ministry, as I did. However, for those of us who are, we can face some real challenges. I had been taught that to be the right kind of Christian woman, I needed to stay home and take care of the cooking and cleaning, just as I had always done. It took time for me to discover that God did not expect this of me, nor did my family. It was only the manmade constraints and traditions of religion and my old mind-set that expected me to do so.

I was blessed by the love and cooperation of my family, which made it possible for me to go out and fulfill the destiny that God had for me. Not every woman has this kind of support at home. Many times, women experience friction and resistance as they transition into their new identity.

For instance, Frank was accustomed to his wife, Lisa, making life comfortable for him. She kept his home clean, did his laundry, and prepared his meals. She was available for him at all times. When someone asked Lisa what her ministry was, she answered, "My ministry is taking care of Frank." How noble that sounded—and how comforting to Frank!

But Lisa came to a point in her life in which she fell desperately in love with Jesus. Previously, she had been only a nominal Christian. Now, the more she fell in love with Jesus, the more she realized that He had a destiny for her beyond cooking and doing laundry.

Although Lisa continued to take care of her home responsibilities, she began to add other things to her agenda. Soon she was leading a Bible study, and women began calling her for counsel and prayer. As a result, Frank started feeling rejected. Who was this woman he was living with? Where had his former wife gone?

It took God's grace, as well as lots of communication and time, for Frank and Lisa to move together into a new season in their lives. Both had to make adjustments so that their relationship could remain strong. Lisa finally hired a housekeeper and took Frank's clothing to a nearby laundry. Whenever possible, others took over some of her ministry responsibilities so that she could spend time with her husband. In addition, Lisa included Frank in her counseling and prayer ministry, as he understood men and was able to bring a different perspective into the situation.

Working through family dynamics is not easy. The busier you get, the more you have to work at balancing family and ministry. But be assured that the Lord will give you the wisdom you need to find that balance. He does not want you to lose your family due to ministry. And believe me, I speak from experience! I constantly have to work at doing this. Dale and I are exceptionally family-oriented, and now that our children are grown and we have been blessed with several grandchildren, we *really* work at maintaining that necessary balance between ministry and family.

Holidays and birthdays have always been important to us. Now, we schedule them in the same way that we schedule checkups at the dentist. Although we cannot always celebrate birthdays on the actual date, we do celebrate them. I am grateful to have such a wonderful family. They have sacrificed a lot to enable me to get into my destiny, and with God's help and guidance, I am able to show my gratitude and love to them. If you will let Him, the Lord will also show you how to balance family and ministry as you transition into your true identity.

Jealousy from other women is another challenge that we sometimes face when our identity changes. Not everyone will be excited about our call from God or our choice to answer that call. We see that illustrated so clearly in the Bible when Joseph told his brothers about the vision he had received from the Lord:

Then Joseph had a dream, and when he told it to his brothers, they hated him even more (Gen. 37:5).

I once had to deal with a situation involving jealousy when I was asked to be the president of a women's organization. In fact, I was quite surprised when the leadership asked me to take this position, for though I truly loved the Lord and His people, I was fairly new in the things of the Spirit at the time. Yet those making the decision—and God as well—must have overlooked my struggles with fear and insecurity, because not only did they ask me to take the position, but I also knew that God was giving me the green light to accept.

> *Sometimes, you will find yourself the target of a jealous spirit simply because God is moving you forward and putting His favor upon you.*

However, it wasn't long after I assumed my new leadership role that a lady who had previously been in that position attempted suicide. We later learned that she had wanted the position again, and jealousy had driven her to a desperate act. I was shocked and dismayed, and yet I had no reason to feel guilty or responsible for her behavior. I hadn't done anything to put myself in that leadership position. I had been asked, and because I felt God's urging to accept, I had done so. Yet when this incident occurred, I wondered if I should resign.

An inner struggle tormented me for the next several days, but the Lord was faithful to show me that I had not caused the situation. Because I wanted to help and not to hurt, I cooked food and took it to this woman's home. I continued to show love in every way that I could, hoping to help bring healing to the woman's life.

Sometimes, you will find yourself the target of a jealous spirit simply because God is moving you forward and putting His favor upon you. In that sort of situation, you must be careful to maintain a humble spirit and let God's love flow through you. And there is something else that will happen when you make a conscious decision to receive a new identity from the Lord: He will give you a new name. Let me give you an example from my book *God's Purpose for Your Life*:

> It has been said, "A man is not a man until his father tells him he is a man." We yearn for the affirmation of who we truly are apart from our parents and close relationships. When these people have been unable or unwilling to affirm us, we are not without hope. The Lord is able to speak a healing word and affirm our identity. As we learn to listen for Him to tell us who we really are, the new name brings us out of captivity and establishes us in a new place.
>
> Joshua had been a warrior under the leadership of Moses. As Joshua approached the time for a new season in his life, he needed a new identity. He would no longer be just one of the warriors. No longer would he be able to depend on Moses to make the critical decisions for the nation of Israel. He would now be the leader to take a nation into its destiny. Joshua needed a new name to empower him to fulfill his call for the new season. Moses, as a spiritual father, changed Joshua's name. "But Moses called Hoshea the son of Nun, Joshua" (Num. 13:16).[1]

Just as Joshua received a new name that corresponded with his new identity, the Lord will do the same for you. Understand that

He may reveal this new name and identity to you in several ways. So listen for the Lord to speak to you. What name does He call you? What are the new names that others are beginning to call you?

You may need to fight the good fight of faith so that you do not forget your new name, particularly when negative circumstances seem to contradict that new name. Share your testimony of overcoming your old name with others in order to secure your victory, and then agree with the Lord's new identity for your life. Patsy Chmelar tells of her journey as she received a new identity from the Lord:

> Several years ago, the Lord spoke to my heart that the spirit of fear had been controlling my life. He showed me all the ways that fear had kept me from getting even close to my destiny. He told me that I would have breakthrough in every area of my life, but that I had to learn how to walk through it.
>
> For the next five years, every kind of fear spirit attacked me. I even had panic attacks for a month. In my despair and pain, I asked God for the strategy to overcome. Many times I became very weary in the battle, but I kept moving forward in this warfare. I knew that I had to change my mind-set from fearful thinking to one in which I believe that "I can do all things through Christ who strengthens me" (Phil. 4:13, *NKJV*).
>
> Then we lost our home of 18 years to toxic mold and had to leave it and everything in it behind. We had nowhere to go and no money to help us get back on our feet, as we were tremendously in debt. My husband and I decided to go to a secluded place so that we could pray, fast and seek the Lord. We began to ask God, "What is

Your plan and purpose for us?" This particular time in our life was like a death. We lost friends and felt completely isolated, but we stayed close to the Lord.

The panic attacks began just prior to losing our home, and I soon became very mad at the enemy. I began declaring that he would have to give back seven times what he had stolen from me and not take another thing.

God gave me key Scriptures to proclaim and declare. I read every Scripture that I could find on the words "fear," "afraid," "oppression," "dread," "worry," "anxiety," and other negatives. One of my favorite verses was 2 Timothy 1:7: "For God has not given us a spirit of fear, but of power and of love and of a sound mind" (*NKJV*). That Scripture changed my life. Sometimes I began to feel as if I was losing my mind, but I knew that God made me to be an overcomer.

When I changed my mind-set from defeat to victory, things really started happening. As my husband and I left our place of seclusion and prayer, God spoke into my spirit, "Things are not as they seem. The ball is already rolling for your future." That very day, a cousin called with a place for us to stay, rent-free, for several months. That was the beginning. People gave us money and clothes. It never was a huge amount, but just what we needed to make it through the day. God then brought a businessman into our lives who we thought was going to buy our business. Instead, this man gave us a beautiful, huge home and a new vehicle.

As I began the battle to overcome fear, God revealed to me that I would be traveling with Barbara Wentroble. I couldn't see how that would ever happen, because I was just little ole me in a small town in Texas, and I didn't have the confidence to do anything like that. But the Lord gave me the strategy to overcome, and then the choice was up to me.

Almost two years ago, my daughter and I were part of Barbara's team that went to Costa Rica to minister to abused women. Barbara gave a message on receiving our new identity and said that God has a new name for us. "You shall be called by a new name, which the mouth of the Lord will name" (Isa. 62:2, *NKJV*). Barbara had us reject and refuse our old name and explained that our new name would lead us to our destiny. God revealed to me that my old name was *fear*, and then showed me that my new name would be *bold*. I accepted that new name and began to walk in that boldness!

The enemy will do anything he can to keep us from our destiny, but God will do everything He can to help us get there. Don't give up in your battle. Your victory may be just around the corner!

Along the journey toward your new identity, you may need to deal with other issues in your life. Some of these issues may include fears or other hindrances designed to prevent you from reaching your destiny. Although these issues may seem too big to overcome, God will give you the strategy to break through every obstacle. In the next chapter, we will look at various ways in which God will come alongside us and empower us for this exciting journey.

Discussion Questions

1. Explain any struggle you have experienced as a result of "identity theft."

2. What are some of the ways you have been helped in discovering and transitioning into your true identity?

3. What is the old name that identified you?

4. Has the Lord given you a new name? If so, what is it?

5. Describe the ways you have been fighting the good fight of faith to secure your new name.

Note

1. Barbara Wentroble, *God's Purpose for Your Life* (Ventura, CA: Regal Books, 2002), p. 109.

Dealing with Fears and Hindrances

Marianne endured more loss in the early years of her childhood than most of us experience in a lifetime. When she was two years old, she lost her only sibling. Although Marianne was too young to understand what happened, she became a very frightened and sad little girl who cried most of the time. Then, when she was eight, her parents told her that she was going to have a new little brother or sister. Marianne was very excited and dared to hope that something good was about to happen in her life. Instead, the much-anticipated baby was stillborn, and Marianne's mother died from complications in childbirth.

Marianne was devastated and began clinging to her father incessantly. Her father, however, soon decided that he wasn't able to care for his frightened daughter, so he sent her to live with an aunt and uncle she scarcely knew. This couple had no children of their own, and the reason for this soon became apparent to Marianne: Her new guardians did not like children. When they decided three months later that they didn't want Marianne anymore, they shipped her off to live with her maternal grandparents.

Her grandparents cared for her physical needs, but they seemed unable to comprehend the emotional needs of a little girl who felt that she had lost everyone and been rejected by all those whom she had ever loved.

When Marianne grew up and married, she was so fearful of losing her new family that she clung to her husband and children to the point of nearly smothering them. Every decision she made in her waking hours was driven and governed by fear. When she finally fell asleep, nightmares of abandonment prevented her from getting any real rest. It wasn't until she was 50 years old and finally came to know Jesus Christ as her Savior that she began to experience God's perfect love that drives out fear. Now, at age 84, she acknowledges that God has brought her a long way on her journey from fear to faith. She now knows that she is wrapped in the safety of His promise to never leave or forsake her.

Fear. If we let it, it will wrap its ugly tentacles around us and choke out the very life that God has breathed into us. Fear is one of the most common obstacles that keep women from fulfilling their God-appointed destiny.

I used to be a registered nurse, so when I heard the old saying about a man with an ulcer, "It's not what the man is eating; it's what's eating the man," it caught my attention. At the time, many of the modern medicines that are used today for treating ulcers were not available. I remember working in the Intensive Care Unit of hospitals and seeing patients suffering from bleeding ulcers. There were times when no amount of medicine, surgery or blood transfusions could save their lives. The eating away of the stomach lining as a result of the ulcer caused the life in these patients to drain away.

I have never personally experienced an ulcer, but I did experience the internal eating away of my life so that the real life in me was impotent. Today, I am a miracle of God's love, grace and healing power. But one of the emotional ulcers that ate away at me was fear. I didn't merely experience one fear; I had several, and each one had major effects on my life.

The greatest fear I probably ever experienced was what I now know as the "fear of man," meaning mankind. For most of my life, I was not aware that I even had that fear. Can you believe it? The reason I didn't know that I had this fear was because I had lived with it my entire life and had come to believe that it was normal for me. Often, we can find ourselves in bondage and not realize it because we accept the way we are as just being part of our personality. Without our conscious acquiescence, we actually come into agreement with the enemy's plan for our lives rather than God's plan.

As a young adult, I attended a women's conference and heard the speaker make a statement that forever changed my life: "You will never walk in the fear of the Lord until you lose the fear of man." Her words were like arrows into my heart. The fear of man! Could this be what was causing me to feel bashful, timid and intimidated? That thought had never before entered my mind.

That night began a new journey for me: A journey out of bondage and into freedom. Up until that life-changing experience, my voice would literally close off when I was asked to speak to more than three people. No matter how hard I tried, I could not get one sound to come out of my mouth!

After realizing my problem, I began to recall fearful situations from my past. I remembered times from my school days when I was afraid to raise my hand and answer the teacher's question for fear that I might be wrong and humiliate myself in front of my classmates. And getting up to speak in front of my classmates was absolutely out of the question.

During my first year of nursing school, I discovered that freshmen were required to take a public speaking class. I had to give two-minute, five-minute and ten-minute speeches, and though I received an *A* in the class, I hated every minute of it. My inner turmoil before each speech was overwhelming. I felt that I was a complete failure. Interestingly, the school only used that course for my freshman class. The next year, they reverted to teaching Freshman English, which I would have greatly preferred. Looking back, however, I see the hand of the Lord in that situation, even though at the time I thought it was an assignment from hell.

After hearing the speaker at that women's conference say that we cannot walk in the fear of the Lord until we get rid of the fear of man, I made a decision. More than anything else, I wanted the fear of the Lord in my life. I truly wanted to please the Lord more than I wanted to please people. So I decided that I would do whatever it took to be free of the fear of man. If that meant making a mistake in front of others, I would do it. If it meant looking foolish and being wrong in public when I was trying to please the Lord, I would do it.

The Holy Spirit helped me overcome and break free of this lifelong bondage. From the night I made that firm decision to walk in the fear of the Lord, the Holy Spirit was always there to remind me of that decision. Each time I attempted to speak to a group and sensed the grip of fear around my throat, I also sensed the voice of the Lord asking me, "Barbara, is this the fear of the Lord or the fear of man?" I then had to make a choice. "I choose the fear of the Lord," I would answer firmly.

My fear did not go away immediately. Sometimes the Lord performs an instant miracle, but at other times (as we saw in the previous chapter), He takes us through a process. Miracles do happen, but they are not the ordinary way that God works.

God's process is the norm. My process took several years, yet each time I chose the fear of the Lord instead of the fear of man, I came into a new level of freedom. I was determined to be free of the fear of man, and I had to persevere by continually choosing the fear of the Lord over a period of time until I was free.

Another fear that plagued me in my life was the fear of heights. One time when I attended camp as a child, I was unable to climb the steps of the fire ranger's tower. I would climb a few steps, but then fear would grip me and prevent me from continuing. So I would carefully back down the steps to the ground.

After talking with many women through the years, I discovered that I was not alone in this particular fear. I have met many people who will not use elevators with glass walls. This fear of heights limits and restricts where people can go and what they can accomplish.

Miracles do happen, but they are not the ordinary way God works—God's process is the norm.

My husband and I once helped move a missionary family to Mexico. As we wound through the mountains along narrow roads, my fear of heights assaulted me until my stomach felt so sick that I could not eat. In fact, I could barely drink anything during the three-day trip.

After staying awake through the last night of the journey, I climbed into the car, dreading another day of riding through the mountains. *Surely, if I read Psalm 91, I will be okay*, I thought. Yet I was able to read only a few verses before I had to stop because I was crying so hard that it was impossible to see the page.

"Lord, if You don't do something, I don't know what I'll do," I cried. I closed the Bible and leaned my head back on the seat of the car for about 15 minutes. As I came to a place of giving up on anything that I could do to overcome my fear, the Lord suddenly worked a miracle in my life. I realized that I had to cast this fear completely on the Lord, and as I did, I felt something break off my left shoulder.

It was such a powerful sensation that I sat up in my seat. I didn't know what had happened until I looked out the window and saw majestic mountains covered with tall, beautiful trees and powerful waterfalls cascading down the sides. "Lord," I exclaimed, "You made all this for us to enjoy!" I was amazed that the very things that had brought terror to me just 15 minutes earlier had now become objects of beauty! Jesus had truly set me free.

There will be times when we have done everything that we have been taught to do to come into freedom, and yet nothing seems to work. We have worshiped; we have quoted Scripture; we have meditated on the Lord and His promises. It is at this point that we, like the prodigal son, come to the end of ourselves. We know that there is nothing more that we can do, so we finally give up and hand our fears, insecurities, rejection or any other hindrances to the Lord and allow His presence to heal and deliver us.

You may not feel a physical sensation when this happens as I did, but you will know that you are free. Fear will be gone. Panic will no longer have power over you. Situations will look and feel different. Life will have changed.

Whatever is hindering you from fulfilling God's plan for your life, you need to give up trying to fix it yourself, because you can't. Give it to God. Invite His presence to wrap you in His love and let Him break the power of your captivity.

Today, I frequently minister to people who live high up in the mountains in other nations. As I watch young people in these nations worship the Lord with tears streaming down their face and sing, "There's gonna be a revival in our land," I remember the Lord's goodness to set me free from my fear of heights. Had He not done this, I could not have fulfilled my destiny.

You may not be called to go to the mountains of another country. Yet you may be called to go on a trip to the mountains with your family. You may want to view cities from tall skyscrapers. You may be asked to speak at a PTA meeting or at your workplace. Ask the Lord to break your captivity to fear so that you can do whatever He has planned for you to do in your life.

During those years of struggle, I didn't know that the Lord was preparing me for my destiny. I didn't know that He would send me to the nations of the world to speak prophetically into the lives of government and business leaders. I didn't know that He would have me speaking at large conferences and raising up leaders. Too often, we limit ourselves by viewing life through a small lens, while the Lord sees the big picture of the destiny He has planned for us.

The fear of man and the fear of heights were only two of the fears in my life. Through the years, the Lord has broken me out of every fear (see Ps. 34:4). Each time He did so, I first had to recognize that I had a fear and call it by name before I could come into freedom. As long as I accepted my fear or just labeled it as part of my personality, I could not be free from the fear. The first step in problem solving is always to recognize that we have a problem.

Once I recognized the problem, the next step that I had to take was to forgive others. The Lord helped me to realize that deep inside I held on to unforgiveness toward people who had vented anger toward me, said hurtful words to me, or done other things to me that opened me up to some of these fears. Each time I remembered one of these situations, I would consciously say, "Lord, I forgive." More than once, I had to choose to speak out forgiveness for the same person. However, I kept willfully forgiving until I felt total release inside.

> *We must choose to forgive, just as we must choose to allow God to set us free from fear.*

Forgiving someone is a choice. Not forgiving someone is also a choice, and it carries deadly consequences. Holding on to unforgiveness is a lot like drinking poison and then waiting for the other person to die. It simply doesn't work that way. We must choose to forgive, just as we must choose to allow God to set us free from fear. In order to do that, we must first address our fears and command them to turn us loose. We must then pray and commit our fears to God. Here is one sample prayer that you can pray to release the fears in your life:

Father, I come to you in the powerful name of Jesus. Your name is more powerful than the name of fear. I am your daughter. You have given me authority to rule in the earth [see Gen. 1:26-28]. Today, I take that authority and rule over fear. I command every form of fear to turn me loose in the name of Jesus! Fear has no right over me since I am the Temple of the Holy Spirit.

I break the power of fear that has come to me through the generations in my family. I renounce all past involvement with occult powers in my life or in the life of my family. Jesus is Lord of my life, and I will serve only Him.

I ask that the Holy Spirit fill every place in me where there has been fear. Make me a sanctuary for Your Presence. Thank

You for setting me free. Thank You for filling me with Your Holy Spirit. Remind me not to allow fear to have access in my life from this day forth.

In Jesus' name I pray. Amen.

Fear was one area of my life that I had to deal with in order to come into the fullness of God's plan for my life. However, I ran into many other hindrances along the way that I also had to learn how to overcome. One of those main hindrances was my own mind-set. I was convinced that others were more intelligent and more spiritual than I was, and that mind-set produced inordinate insecurity within me.

When I first began speaking, it was only at a few small meetings. One time, as I was preparing to go to one of those meetings, I received a call. A woman, who seemed light years ahead of me spiritually, told me that she felt the Lord leading her to go to the meeting with me. She continued by saying that the Lord had revealed to her that while I was ministering to people, He would show *her* a "black spot" on the person I was ministering to, which indicated the location of a demon. I was so new in the Spirit that this overwhelmed me. I was sure that I needed this woman, because I couldn't imagine the Lord showing me something like that, even though I was the speaker.

The woman joined me at the meeting, but she failed to see any black spots. However, as I ministered to people, I found that God was faithful to reveal to me whatever I needed to know. It took time before I realized that my insecurity left me vulnerable to being used by someone who wanted to open the door to his or her own ministry. I didn't realize that the Lord was trying to get me to rise up out of insecurity. He wanted me to depend on Him rather than on other people.

The Lord will bring mentors and teachers into your life. However, these people are not to take the place of leaning on the Lord and learning to hear His voice. Reading Scripture and meditating on what God's Word says can help you break old mind-sets. Put your name in the Scriptures. I like to do that to personalize the Scriptures for any situation I am facing. For example, "Barbara is not to be conformed to this world, but is to be transformed by the renewing of her mind, so that Barbara may prove what is the good, acceptable and perfect will of God" (see Rom. 12:2).

One of the hindrances that you may be facing is the belief that you are too old and have missed God's opportunity for your life. My friend Jean Hodges wrote of her experience with this hindrance in *God's Bold Call to Women:*

> For many years as a pastor's wife, I sat on the pew, not really seeing myself as a minister. I taught Sunday School and led prayer meetings and the women's ministry, yet I did not really embrace the call to the ministry that I had received at the age of 16. . . . God has a timetable for our lives, but many times we think we have missed it or we can't do it. Fear, intimidation, discouragement and the words "you can't" hold us captive and immobile. God is saying: "You can, and you will!" He is removing the cultural burkas, the cocoons that have held us captive. His word is working in us to produce faith![1]

Jean went on to describe the way she received several prophetic words over her life during a period of a few years. She wrote that the Lord puts a seed of His Word in our lives but that we must water, cultivate, believe and act on the Word for it to grow. As Jean was faithful to do this, God began to open doors for her to minister.

Whether you are bound by fear, insecurity, unforgiveness or other hindrances, the plan of the enemy is the same: to keep you from fulfilling God's call on your life. How wonderful is God's plan for us—and how sad if we miss it! His Spirit can empower us to overcome every fear, and His power can cause us to dismantle every hindrance.

You are not today who you will be tomorrow, but you are becoming the woman God created you to be. Go forth in His power and refuse to allow any fear or hindrance stop God's plan for your life!

Now that you are being released from fears, insecurities and other hindrances, you are ready to stand side by side with men. This convergence will help bring God's will to the earth. In the next chapter, we will take a look at this powerful convergence.

Discussion Questions

1. What is the name of the greatest fear in your life? (Be honest!)

   - Call the fear by name.
   - Take authority over the fear and tell it that it no longer has power in your life.
   - Ask the Holy Spirit to remind you if you are tempted to yield to the old fear.
   - Command your will to choose the will of God for your life.
   - Take faith actions to break the power of the fear—run *into* the fear rather than *from* it.
   - Ask the Lord to wrap you in His love.
   - Rest in His love and listen to what He says.

2. Name at least one area of hindrance or insecurity in your life.

   - How have you dealt with the hindrance in your past?
   - Why did you deal with it that way?
   - What were the results of that action?
   - What do you need to change so that you can come into freedom?

3. Do you think of yourself as being too old or too young for God's destiny for your life?

- Name an older person who has had an impact on your life in a positive way. What did that person do?
- Name a young person who touched your life in a positive way. What did that person do?

4. What are you waiting for?

Notes

1. Jean Hodges, quoted in Barbara J. Yoder, *God's Bold Call to Women* (Ventura, CA: Regal Books, 2005), pp. 78-79.

Partnership of Men and Women

"You did what?" I asked Dan and Wilma in disbelief. Inside, I asked myself, *How could they have done such a thing?*

I had known Dan and Wilma for some time and they seemed to be levelheaded, solid church members. They had joined the church shortly after my husband, Dale, and I began pastoring, and I had witnessed with my own eyes how they loved the Lord, were faithful in attendance, displayed strong leadership abilities, and were willing to help anytime the church needed a volunteer. Their decision seemed completely out of character for them, but as they sat in my office telling me their story, I realized how incorrect religious teachings can produce unwise decisions and unnecessary problems, particularly in a marriage.

Wilma worked as the bookkeeper for a roofing company in our city. She was well-respected and did a superb job for her employer. Dan worked in real estate and won the hearts of many people with his outgoing personality. He was truly a people person. Somewhere along the line, they began attending a discipling program that was led by a man who was not a member of our church. Now this discipling program was having a negative effect on Dan and Wilma's marriage.

The man had told them that Dan was the head of the family and that he should therefore be handling all the family's finances. In obedience to this teaching, Wilma released the checkbooks and turned the financial responsibilities over to Dan, who had no training or experience in this area. However, he too wanted to be obedient to the Lord, so he reasoned that if obeying God meant that he had to write the checks, pay all the bills and balance the budget, he would do it. So even though Wilma was an expert bookkeeper and Dan was completely inexperienced in finances, they made the transition.

It was only a matter of months before financial problems developed. The electric company called to notify them that the electricity would be turned off in a few days because Dan had not paid the electric bill. Days later, the water department notified Dan and Wilma that they would be disconnecting service due to failure to pay the water bill. Wilma was stunned. She knew that there were sufficient funds in the bank to cover the utility bills. What was the problem?

As I mentioned, Dan loved people, which helped him become very successful in real estate. The problem was that Dan became so involved with people that he forgot to pay the family bills, particularly since this was something he wasn't used to doing. Incorrect religious teaching had forced Dan into a place for which God had not gifted him nor in which He intended for him to function, and the results were alarming.

After I shared with Dan and Wilma the truth of God's Word concerning the partnership of men and women, they made the necessary adjustments. Dan happily returned the checkbook and bills to Wilma, which freed him to once again spend time with people, sell real estate and be the successful man that God intended him to be. Wilma could now relax, knowing the bills were paid and the bank account was balanced. The friction in their marriage disappeared, because they were both now happily doing what God had gifted them to do.

I have often observed similar situations in marriages. Manmade religious rules put requirements on men and women that are not required by the Lord. Nothing in the Bible says that a man is supposed to handle the finances in a marriage.

God always intended for men and women to walk together in partnership and fulfill His purpose in the earth. The Bible teaches that both men and women were created in God's image. They both have a direct relationship with God. Both are to share together the responsibilities of bearing and rearing children and having dominion over the created order (see Gen. 1:26-28).

Women were designed by God to be helpers to men. Often, this word is interpreted to mean that women are inferior to men and are to be in a subservient position. However, the word "helper" in Hebrew is the word *ezer*. Strong's Concordance says that the word means "to protect or to aid . . . succour."[1] This is the same word that is used many times in Scripture to describe God as our helper. Since we know that God is not inferior or subservient to men and that women as well as men were made in God's image, we know that women are not inferior or subservient to men. Women were created as equals with men, sharing in the assignment of ruling and having dominion in the earth.

> *M*en and women were created for full and equal partnership. It was never God's plan to have one gender rule over the other.

God planned for there to be interdependence between men and women. Restoration must therefore return both genders to their pre-Fall position. Ed Silvoso addressed this idea in his book *Women, God's Secret Weapon:*

> In the Garden, Adam was created first, and as such, he was given a role as a protector when God handed down the prohibition not to eat from the tree. But it is also true that Adam by himself was "not good" (Gen. 2:18). It was Eve's creation that enabled *both* of them to rule over all creation since the command was not given until after she was created. In Genesis 1:28, the Hebrew verb commanding Adam and Eve to rule over the creation is *plural*—it is a command given to both the man and the woman, which means that the woman rules alongside her husband (see also Gen. 2:18).[2]

Throughout the Old Testament, we find women who were used by the Lord even before Jesus came with His redemption. If God used women in the Old Testament, how much more does He desire to use them after redemption as New Covenant believers! Some of the women God used for His purposes in the Old Testament were:

- *Sarah.* Sarah is known as the "mother of faith." Due to her faithfulness to God, her name was later changed from Sarai to Sarah when part of God's Name, Jehovah, was added to her name (see Gen. 17:15).

- *Miriam.* Miriam served as a leader in partnership with Moses and Aaron. She was considered an elder in her nation (see Mic. 6:4).

• *Deborah.* Deborah was a prophet who knew the will of God for her nation. She led both men and women. In fact, a man by the name of Barak refused to go to war without her. He was not a weak man who had to depend on a woman—gender was not the issue! He simply would not go to war without someone who knew what God was saying, and he knew that Deborah heard from God. Under Deborah's leadership, Israel experienced 40 years of peace, the longest period of peace for the nation under any of the judges (see Judg. 4-5).

• *Huldah.* Huldah lived during the time when the nation of Israel was backslidden and involved with false religion. When a man found the scrolls of God's Word, he brought them to King Josiah, who sent for Huldah to interpret them (see 2 Kings 22:14). Huldah had her own seminary and understood God's Word. When others were backslidden, she still had the passion of God. She prophesied and moved in spiritual authority.

• *Esther.* Esther also moved in spiritual authority within the sphere of government, even to the point of laying her own life on the line. Her strategic wisdom and willingness to sacrifice her life caused her own people to be saved, and the enemy was destroyed (see Esther 4-7).

As you can see, men and women were created for full and equal partnership. It was never God's plan to have one gender rule over the other. As we saw previously, Jesus always taught that all believers are necessary and beneficial to the Body of Christ. At Pentecost, the Holy Spirit came upon men and women alike, and both were given gifts without discrimination (see Acts 2:1-21; 1 Cor. 12:7,11; 14:31). Men and women are called by the Lord to develop and exercise those gifts as good stewards of the grace of God.

Jesus came to redeem women as well as men. Through faith in Christ, we all become children of God. We are one in Christ, and we share as heirs of the blessings of salvation. In Christ, there are no distinctions with regard to racial, social or gender bias (see John 1:12-13; Rom. 8:14-17, 2 Cor. 5:17; Gal. 3:26-28).

Early in 2002, shortly after the United States invaded Afghanistan to launch the War on Terrorism, I made my first trip to Afghanistan to help lead a team for humanitarian relief. While I was there serving the Afghan people, I was greatly affected by the extent of the enemy's hatred toward women. Nearly every one of the women in that country wore a burka, a heavy blue covering that allowed for nothing but their eyes to show through.

When I talked with these women, I learned that some of them were teachers and lawyers, but under the male-dominated Taliban regime, they had been forced to quit their jobs and stay home. I also learned that young girls were forbidden from receiving an education. Women under that system experienced oppression, physical abuse and even sexual mutilation—all done in compliance with their religious regulations. In such cultures, women are often suppressed, held back from their full potential, put under male domination, and told that they must stay in their "place."

No matter the culture, the woman's place often is seen as a subservient position, with the man as her "head." The man is referred to as the head of the home, which is consequently interpreted to mean that he is the ruler of the home. I do not want to go into a full discussion here of the teaching concerning men and their rule over women, as many books have already been written on the subject, but I do want to provide a couple of examples to clarify the meaning of "head" in relation to marriage. There are only two references in the Bible that refer to the "headship" of the husband. The first instance is in 1 Corinthians 11:3: "But I want you to know that the head of every man is Christ, the head of woman is man, and the head of Christ is God" (*NKJV*). The other instance is found in Ephesians 5:23: "For the husband is head of the wife, as also Christ is head of the church; and He is the Savior of the body" (*NKJV*).

Genesis 3:16 refers to the consequences of the Fall, rather than the will of God. Whenever a man or woman walks contrary to the grace of God, he or she will always desire preeminence and will always have the desire to rule. When the grace of God works in the heart of a man, he loses the love of preeminence and the desire to rule over his wife. When God's grace works in the heart of a woman, she loses the desire to rule over her husband.

Jesus, as the Head of the Church, is our example of what "headship" is to be like. "The stone which the builders rejected, this became the chief cornerstone" (Matt. 21:42). The cornerstone gives support to the building. It also binds the sides of the building together. Therefore, Jesus, as Head of the Church, is also the support of the Church and binds its members together (see Eph. 4:15-16; Col. 2:19).

Note that although Ephesians 4:15 and Colossians 2:19 describe Christ as the Head, neither of these Scriptures speak of His government. Instead, these Scriptures portray Him as the support, nourisher and builder of the Body. The head, therefore, is also the source. When we speak of the headwaters of a river, we are describing the source of that water. In the same way, the head of the home is the source of life.

This term was never intended to indicate government or authority. The husband is to be the source of life in the home.

Like Jesus, he is to be a support, nourisher and builder of the family. In addition, when the Bible teaches that a woman (or wife) is to submit to her husband, it is not referring to subjection or forced servitude. The biblical meaning of "submission" is "to willingly come underneath in a safe place."

In the military, privates submit to sergeants, sergeants submit to lieutenants, and lieutenants submit to captains, majors and generals because it creates a safe and orderly system. The onus, however, is not on the private to protect and cover but rather on those who serve above the private, even as Jesus protects and covers His Church and requires a husband to protect and cover his wife. This enables the husband and wife to fight the good fight together and to experience the victory as equals.

Throughout the New Testament, Jesus lifts up His Church to sit with Him in heavenly places and share in His rulership over the earth. The Church is not subjected under His feet, as are the principalities and powers, but is designed to share in His rule. Jesus gives us a picture of Himself and the Church so that we can understand how men and women are to be in partnership. As fellow disciples of the Lord, both men and women are to treat their partners as Jesus instructed in the Scriptures:

> You know that the rulers of the Gentiles lord it over them, and their great men exercise authority over them. It is not this way among you, but whoever wishes to become great among you shall be your servant (Matt. 20:25-26; see also Luke 22:25-26).

One couple who has learned to walk together in partnership

is Melanie and Woody Blok of Sri Lanka. Melanie and Woody live in a culture that oppresses women and requires them to live in a subordinate position to men. However, they have chosen to live according to the culture of the kingdom of God rather than the culture of their earthly country.

Melanie married Woody and moved to Sri Lanka after graduating from Bible School. Although she did not grow up in a ministry home, she understood that because Woody pastored a church, she would face many unique challenges as a pastor's wife in a different culture. Many of the members of Emmanuel Church, which Woody and Melanie pastor, come from Buddhist, Hindu or Catholic backgrounds. Spiritual leaders in these religions do not marry, so although the new converts received Melanie warmly, they were hesitant about her role as a woman leader.

After Melanie began to share the pulpit with her husband, word spread throughout the community that she was preaching. Other pastors in the city made negative comments about Melanie to her husband. However, Woody was delighted to have his wife minister alongside him. He was willing to go against the culture and religious mind-sets of his country.

In a South Asian culture in which women are often oppressed, Woody is not threatened by women in leadership. Women in his church now serve communion and preach on occasion. Some serve as board members and deacons in his church, and some have even been ordained. Women leaders in this church are helping to break down the wall of division between men and women. They are walking in partnership together, in spite of the culture in that region.

Walls of division that have prevented men and women from walking in full partnership are crumbling, even as the walls of Eastern Europe started falling in the 1980s. Jesus came to tear down *every* dividing wall. "For He Himself is our peace, who made both groups into one and broke down the barrier of the dividing wall" (Eph. 2:14).

In his book *The Three Prejudices*, Kelly Varner writes the following regarding God's plan for men and women to walk together in partnership:

> God's ultimate intention is for man and woman to be *one* within the rent veil, within the Most Holy Place, the place of Jesus' finished work. When the will of man is one with the will of his God, and the will of woman is one with the will of her God, their name or nature becomes one. Authority and submission is then swallowed up in singleness and union—the will of man and woman harmonize in complete agreement with the Lord. Two become one in the purest and fullest sense of the word.[3]

A tsunami of God's Spirit is crumbling every wall that keeps men and women from fulfilling His purpose.

God is indeed empowering a new generation of men and women to walk side by side and move into every area of life with great victory. A shift has taken place in the earth. A tsunami of God's Spirit is crumbling every wall that keeps men and women from fulfilling His purpose. Together, men and women are arising in partnership to bring transformation in the nations of the earth!

Not only has God called women to walk in partnership with men, but He has also called women to positions of leadership. Women leaders are arising today to their God-given destinies. In the next chapter, we will examine how some of these women have answered God's call to leadership in their lives.

Discussion Questions

1. Name several religious teachings that have caused you to believe that God called man (the male gender) to rule over you.

2. What are some of the difficulties you have experienced as you have tried to live according to these teachings? What did you do to overcome those difficulties?

3. How would you define the husband as head of the wife?

4. How would you define Jesus as head of the Church?

5. Describe the difference in the two "heads," according to your theological understanding.

6. What is your understanding of the term "helper," in regard to a woman being her husband's helper?

Notes

1. James Strong, *The Exhaustive Concordance of the Bible, Hebrew and Chaldee Dictionary* (McLean, VA: MacDonald Publishing Company, n.d.), Hebrew #5828.
2. Ed Silvoso, *Women, God's Secret Weapon* (Ventura, CA: Regal Books, 2001), p. 117.
3. Kelley Varner, *The Three Prejudices* (Shippensburg, PA: Destiny Image Publishers, Inc., 1997), p. 46.

Women in Leadership

By 2004, I had made several trips to the nation of Afghanistan, where I witnessed firsthand the second-class citizenship and shabby treatment of women. So it was with great excitement one day when I viewed the picture on the front page of the newspaper. There, in living color, was a photo that exemplified the transformation Afghanistan had experienced since the arrival of American troops less than three years earlier, which had spurred the removal of the tyrannical and oppressive rule of the Taliban. Seeing that country's first female presidential candidate, Massouda Jalal, standing beside a mosque and urging a mostly male audience to vote for her during the October elections made me want to jump up and down and cheer in triumph. As one reporter commented:

> In Afghanistan, presidential candidates, male or female, never existed until a few months ago. Such were the barriers between sexes in this deeply conservative society—women risked beating or death if they stood in front of men inside mosques, much less spoke to them.[1]

The reporter went on to add that perhaps the greatest evidence of change was in the men's reaction when candidate Massouda Jalal delivered her speech. They clapped and cheered repeatedly as the courageous candidate broke new ground by giving campaign speeches inside mosques and at rallies in villages where women still needed their husbands' permission to register to vote.[2]

Leadership by women has been a controversial issue since Adam and Eve first sinned and broke fellowship with God. Yet, despite the Fall and its resulting curse, the Bible is filled with examples of women leaders. Throughout both the Old and New Testaments, Scripture reveals the Lord's desire to use women as leaders. "The Lord gives the word [of power]; the women who bear and publish [the news] are a great host" (Ps. 68:11, *AMP*).

Women leaders have always been used, to one extent or another, in the Church as well as in society. However, many have paid a price to obey the Lord's call to leadership. These brave women have cleared a path so that many more can follow and do mighty exploits for the Lord. Today, Christian women are entering every arena of leadership. They are involved in government, education, the arts, medicine, church, business and professional fields.

Obeying the call of God to the workplace is not always comfortable. Sandra, who lives in the Midwest, told the following story of how she was dragged, kicking and screaming against the will of God, into a political career:

When I began working as a deputy in a county office, I was hired with the understanding that I was being trained to become the elected official for that office. The more I watched politics from the inside, the more I decided that I didn't want to be a politician. From what I could see, politicians lied, cheated, gossiped and looked for weaknesses that they could exploit. In other words, they acted just like the world. I finally told God, "This is not for me!"

Sandra described the following months as being filled with fear, doubt and anxiety. In the natural, it looked as if she had no chance to win the election. However, about three weeks before the election, she felt that she had shifted from a place of fear to a place of faith. She even began to make faith declarations that she would win.

When the election was over and the ballots counted, Sandra had won 11 of the 15 precincts in her county, tied in 2 precincts, and lost by a mere 9 votes in the other 2 precincts. Sandra now encourages others, particularly those like her who are initially hesitant to move into what God has for them, with these words: "Once Jonah obeyed God, it took only one man to turn a whole city to God!" Because Sandra broke through the so-called glass ceiling of her mind and emotions to step into leadership, she now has the opportunity to use her position as a political leader in her county to bring righteous changes to the people she serves.

The glass ceilings in the minds and emotions of women are those imagined or felt boundaries that keep them from fulfilling their potential as leaders. These glass ceilings are a limitation that is intangible and yet has great power. They can be someone's mind-set, religious teachings, structures within an organization, or wrong connections.

Hebrews 11:35 describes the tenacity and virtue of women willing to stand in faith and serve the Lord: "Women received back their dead by resurrection; and others were tortured, not accepting their release, in order that they might obtain a better resurrection." The Bible gives many examples of women leaders who broke through their own glass ceilings and changed the course of history. Some of the women leaders in the Old Testament that we have already discussed include:

- *Esther*, who served in the government of her nation
- *Deborah*, who led the men and women in Israel as a judge (of all Israel's judges, Deborah is the only one besides Samuel who held the respected position of prophet)
- *Miriam*, who represented the authority of God to the people and spoke for God

Religious teachings often create strong ceilings for women who are under the influence of those teachings. Gerald L. Zelizer wrote an interesting article in *USA Today*, "Time to Break the 'Stained Glass' Ceiling," in which he quoted a man who was his lunch partner and a prominent member in his congregation as saying, "I would rather hire a gay rabbi than a woman as your successor."[3] Zelizer went on to stress the need to bring understanding to people who think like his lunch partner so that female clergy can arise and fulfill their calling. Zelizer believes that when this happens, the believer in the pew will be the ultimate beneficiary.[4]

In chapter 1, I mentioned Anne Graham Lotz, daughter of famed Baptist evangelist Reverend Billy Graham and his wife, Ruth, as an example of one woman who is coloring outside the lines in her own life and ministry. Anne, who is often described as the best preacher in the Graham family, was once invited by the president of Paraguay and his wife to hold a crusade in the city of Asunción. In the early stages of preparation, long before

Anne went to Paraguay, 6,000 women began to pray, each taking one block of that city for Christ, and they also knocked on doors and invited people to come to the crusade. When Anne preached at the 40,000-seat national soccer stadium, thousands responded to the invitation by giving their lives to Jesus.

God is looking for leaders who are gifted to function. He is not concerned with gender, but rather with calling and obedience. Some women are called to positions of leadership in the business world or in various arenas in society. Many of these women leaders are breaking through the glass ceiling in the workplace, but the struggle to obey the call of God on their lives has not always been an easy journey.

> *God* is looking for leaders who are gifted to function. He is not concerned with gender, but rather with calling and obedience.

Betsy is a leader who broke through the glass ceiling in the medical profession. Although her parents did not encourage her in the pursuit of a career, Betsy was in love with the Lord and had a passion for serving Jesus. It was that passion that helped her press through every difficult situation she encountered on her way to fulfilling her dream of becoming a doctor. Betsy has now worked as a physician for 25 years.

Aside from nursing, much of the medical field has historically been a man's profession. Learning to live as a woman in a man's world was not an easy task for Betsy, who relates that she had to overperform to be accepted on equal terms with men. She had to have higher grades in her courses, work harder at every aspect of her training, and go out of her way to build rapport with her professors who were men. There were times during medical school and her two residencies that Betsy questioned the call. When she walked the halls of the hospital at three in the morning and everyone was sleeping, she would ask herself, *Why am I doing this? Why can't I live a normal life?*

Betsy would no sooner ask the question than she would know the answer. She was doing it because of her intense love for Jesus. The Lord knew her future, and she did not. He knew that in the following years, He would send Dr. Betsy into nations to rescue the perishing and care for the dying. He would have her train thousands of believers around the globe to respond in times of crisis. Advancing the kingdom of God throughout the earth was a destiny that the Lord prepared for Dr. Betsy before she was born.

Betsy's testimony speaks of the way she has stayed focused on the presence of the Lord, even as Moses did, drawing on His strength so that she could fulfill her call as a woman leader: "By faith he left Egypt, not fearing the wrath of the king; for he endured, as seeing Him who is unseen" (Heb. 11:27). Crisis will bring out the best or the worst in all of us, particularly leaders. Betsy chose to let the Lord bring out the best in her so she would not miss her destiny. Reflecting back on her last 40 years since answering the call, she writes:

> I see the major ingredient as being a relentless determination to cognitively and deliberately obey God. It's not even been a once-per-decade lightning bolt or megachoice, but rather a lifetime parade of small, sequential, dying-to-self choices.
>
> Grenades thrown into our van in Kabul, gunfire riots in Pakistan, and earthquake aftershocks in Turkey

threatened to derail me from fulfilling God's calling on my life. The nagging temptation to quit frequently hounded me. Yet all of these, in addition to doubts, depression, loneliness and trauma, have been unsuccessful in swaying me from my destiny. I am founded upon the bedrock of the fear of the Lord and have made Him Master of all my choices. I heard the call of God and became a doer of His voice. I am convinced that these light, momentary afflictions are achieving an eternal weight of glory in my life.

Surely, Dr. Betsy endured because she remained focused on He who is invisible, yet faithful and ever-present. You may not be called to leadership in the nations of the world. Your call to leadership may be at your place of employment, at your child's school, or at a civic organization in your community. As a woman, God has gifted you for leadership wherever He sends you.

The Bible defines the function of leadership as the empowerment of others for service, rather than the exercise of power over them:

But Jesus called them to Himself and said, "You know that the rulers of the Gentiles lord it over them, and their great men exercise authority over them. It is not this way among you, but whoever wishes to become great among you shall be your servant" (Matt. 20:25-26).

Women in both the Old and New Testaments were raised up by God to be powerful leaders in their generations. If God used women in the Old Testament as leaders, how much more would He do so in the New Testament days after the outpouring of the

Holy Spirit on the Day of Pentecost! In fulfillment of Joel's prophesy, the Spirit of the Lord was poured out on both men and women to endue them with power from above so that they could do the work God had for them (see Acts 2:1-18).

We've looked at some of the women leaders in the Old Testament. Now let's look at some of the New Testament leaders:

- *Priscilla* was a woman leader who helped launch the apostolic ministry of Apollos (see Acts 18:24-26).

- *Junia* is listed as an apostle (see Rom. 16:6-8). Some commentators try to masculinize this name, but Dr. Leonard Swidler states, "To the best of my knowledge, no commentator on the text until Aegidus of Rome (1245-1316) took the name to be masculine."[5] A great deal of evidence points to the fact that Junia was a woman.

- *Chloe* pastored one of the churches that was under the oversight of the apostle Paul (see 1 Cor. 1:11).

One of the notable women leaders in the twentieth century was Aimee Semple McPherson. Aimee lived at a time when women were not normally accepted in the ministry, yet she kept focused on God's call to leadership and did not allow religious mind-sets or bad publicity to deter her. Some people describe her as a woman born before her time. She was not afraid to be bold and dramatic—there didn't seem to be anything too radical for this woman. If it meant getting the attention of others in order to draw them to the Lord, she was willing to do whatever was necessary.

During Aimee's lifetime, she composed 175 songs, several operas and 13 drama-oratories. She preached thousands of sermons and graduated more than 8,000 ministers from her L.I.F.E. Bible College. She oversaw the building of the famous Angelus Temple during the Great Depression. Her life is a testimony of the call of God on women to become leaders. Aimee was a spiritual pioneer who helped shape the way we demonstrate Christianity today.

Like Aimee, women in leadership today are being used by the Lord to impact every arena of life, both spiritual and secular. As I stated in an earlier chapter, I grew up in a church that did not allow women to preach from the pulpit, govern in the church, or teach men or boys older than 12. However, the two mission organizations for that particular denomination were both named after women leaders.

What would the world look like today if it had not been touched by the life of Susanna Wesley, the mother of reformers John and Charles Wesley? Susanna homeschooled all of her 19 children and taught them to read Greek and Hebrew and to memorize Scripture.

> *W*omen in leadership today are being used by the Lord to impact every arena of life, both spiritual and secular.

Her method of training later inspired her sons to form the Methodist denomination.

And then there was Kathryn Kuhlman, a woman who caused millions to fall in love with the Holy Spirit and receive His miracle-working power. Kathryn fearlessly paid a high price to walk in obedience to the call of God as a woman leader. Her words speak of the heart-cry of women today who also have chosen to follow Jesus as His leaders:

The world called me a fool for having given my entire life to One whom I've never seen. I know exactly what I'm going to say when I stand in His presence. When I look upon that wonderful face of Jesus, I'll have just one thing to say: "I tried." I gave of myself the best I knew how. My redemption will have been perfected when I stand and see Him who made it all possible.[6]

Kathryn's words are a call to us all: Women leaders, arise! The Lord has raised you up for Kingdom purposes. He has gifted you for His purposes. Do not shrink back from the call of God upon your life. You may be one that the Lord has called to the workplace, or to teach your children God's Word, or to travel to faraway lands to preach the gospel. Whatever unique call to leadership that God has placed on your life, allow Him to position you to fulfill that call and inspire other women to follow in your footsteps.

Discussion Questions

1. Describe the glass ceilings that you have experienced as a woman leader.

2. What have you done to remove those ceilings of limitation?

3. How are women leaders allowed to lead in your church?

4. How are women leaders treated in your workplace or place of influence?

5. Discuss the way you handled a difficult situation as a woman leader. What was the result? How would you handle the same situation now?

6. What will the world look like in the future as a result of your leadership?

Notes

1. Tod Robberson, "Social, Economic Changes Sweep Nation as Afghans Prepare to Vote," *The Dallas Morning News* (October 4, 2004), p. 1.
2. Ibid.
3. Gerald L. Zelizer, "Time to Break the 'Stained Glass' Ceiling," *USA Today* (September 16, 2004), p. 11A.
4. Ibid.
5. Charles Trombley, *Who Said Women Can't Teach?* (South Plainfield, NJ: Bridge Publishing Inc., 1985), p. 191.
6. Roberts Liardon, *God's Generals* (Tulsa, OK: Albury Publishing, 1996), p. 306.

Chapter 6

Women in the Workplace

Tiffany has experienced firsthand the miracle-working power of God in her life. She was born with a cleft palate, and after multiple surgeries and years of speech therapy, the doctors told her mother that Tiffany would never be able to speak normally. Apparently, the doctors didn't check with God on that diagnosis. The Lord has healed Tiffany so completely that she now sings with one of the most beautiful and professional voices of anyone that I have ever heard. She knows she has a call of God on her life, and she has ministered in many nations of the world.

Tiffany is also aware that God has called her to the workplace. She understands that she is called to serve wherever the Lord places her, whether that means working at a secular job or singing in a makeshift church building on a faraway mission field. Tiffany also did not sit around waiting for some great door of opportunity to open: After graduating from Bible school and college, she went to work in Dallas for a large telecommunications company. She recognizes that God placed her there and that she has been called to be a light in the corporate workplace.

It did not take long before Tiffany's coworkers saw something different in her life. They realized that she had a purpose for living, a deep love for people and a peace and hope that they themselves did not possess. When people asked her what made her different, she readily and happily told them about the miracle that God had done in her life and about her personal relationship with Jesus Christ. The inquirers then wanted to know if Tiffany would teach them the Bible and show them how they could also have a relationship with the Lord.

Tiffany went to her supervisor and asked to use a meeting room during the lunch hour for one day each week. Because she was an excellent employee and the favor of God was on her, her supervisor granted her request. Her coworkers began attending the weekly Bible studies, and many received Jesus as their Savior, were filled with the Holy Spirit, and experienced healing and deliverance in their lives. This weekly Bible study, called "Ambassadors for Christ," is now recognized by the company as an "Employee Special Interest Group."

Soon, some of Tiffany's coworkers asked her if they could meet one extra day each week for prayer and ministry. Tiffany received permission, and the weekly prayer meetings began. Within a year, the group had outgrown their meeting space. Tiffany requested a larger room, but this time the building manager refused. Tiffany and her group were not dissuaded. They prayed, and before long the manager was transferred to another building and replaced by a new manager, who gave Tiffany one of the largest meeting rooms available (which also happens to be the most beautiful corporate meeting room in the entire company). Tiffany was given permission to put up flyers and announcements throughout the building to advertise the Bible studies and ministry times and invite others to join them. God truly intervened in this situation and caused His purposes to be fulfilled. "He removes kings and establishes kings" (Dan. 2:21).

The report of this wonderful turn of events and God's great favor on Tiffany and her group spread throughout downtown Dallas. People from other businesses heard how lives were being changed in these meetings and started coming to Ambassadors for Christ on their lunch breaks. Soon, other Bible study and prayer groups were springing up around the city.

Several years ago, Ed Silvoso scheduled a "Light the Nation" conference in Dallas. Before the conference, Tiffany took the members of Ambassadors for Christ out on the streets of Dallas to go on prayer walks and hand out tracts during their lunch hour. Most of her group had never heard of doing such a thing, and they weren't even sure what to expect. By the end of the prayer walk, however, even the most reluctant participants were excited and grateful for the opportunity to serve the Lord in such a meaningful way.

Tiffany understands that she is a person called by the Lord to minister in the workplace because she also understands that ministry is for more than the few people who preach from a pulpit in a church building. All believers are called to be ministers, in whatever circumstances and venues God places them. Tiffany became the pastor, or minister, at this telecommunications company. The company provided a building and a room for their meetings and a congregation for her ministry. Because she was their employee, they even paid her salary!

What makes Tiffany different from the traditional church member? What are some characteristics of these marketplace people such as Tiffany? More than anything else, these individuals view the Church in a radically different way than many of their predecessors, who believed ministry could only happen within the four walls of a church building. They also understand that the empowerment of the Holy Spirit in their lives is for ministry to a lost world. They therefore choose not to be *observers of ministry*, but *participants in* ministry.

While some women feel called to the workplace, others find their call in staying home and raising up the next generation of Christians. My daughter-in-law, Britt, is one of these women. She is a university graduate and has worked as a registered dietician for dialysis clinics. Everything Britt does is marked by a spirit of excellence. When God blessed her and my son, Mark, with two beautiful little girls, Kailee and Sylvia, Britt's response to the call to motherhood was no different. Although she has a college education and the ability to bring in a good income, she believes that the Lord has called her to the role of wife and mother. So she has committed herself to fulfilling those roles in her usual excellent manner.

Britt strategically plans her week for involvement with her family. One day is set aside to go to the library. Another day is set aside for music or attending church activities. Britt schedules the daily activities with her girls as if it were a full-time, away-from-home job.

One day I commented to Britt, "You are amazing with those girls. You handle everything so well and are so patient with them."

Britt smiled. "It's not hard when you're doing what you like to do," she said.

Britt is like many Christian women around the world. She knows that the Lord has called her to pour her life into the next generation. She knows that she has been called to raise up mighty men and women of God who will help shape the course of history and extend the kingdom of God. Therefore, she is willing to invest her time, energy and life into fulfilling God's purpose.

I highly commend Britt and the thousands of other women like her who are obeying God's call on their lives by staying at home and ministering to their family. Their call is not a second-class call—it is a truly high calling from the Lord. What we are doing does not determine the level of our call; the level of our call is determined by obeying what the Lord has called us to do!

Unfortunately, a great number of women, both married and single, struggle between the call of God to the workplace and the religious, societal and traditional teachings that tell them that they must stay at home. Some women are in the workplace due to financial struggles in the family, and some are there because they are single moms working to provide for their children. For many of these women, faulty religious teachings heap guilt upon them, making an already difficult situation worse. Others in the workplace may sense that their call, if they really have one, is not as high as the call of those who preach from the pulpit. Women in the workplace definitely battle between doctrines of their churches and their current position at work.

Often, women are taught that the Bible contains mandates from God that they are supposed to stay home and care for their families, regardless of what they may feel on the inside. A common Scripture used as an example of this mandate is the description of the "virtuous wife" in Proverbs 31. However, if we take a closer look at that particular proverb, we discover a woman who is very smart and adept at business:

> What we are doing does not determine the level of our call; the level of our call is determined by obeying what the Lord has called us to do!

She looks for wool and flax
> and works with her hands in delight.
She considers a field and buys it;
> from her earnings she plants a vineyard.
She stretches out her hand to the distaff,
> and her hands grasp the spindle.
She makes linen garments and sells them,
> and supplies belts to the tradesmen (vv. 13,16,19,24).

In his book *10 Lies the Church Tells Women,* author J. Lee Grady states the following regarding this issue:

> Traditionalists who champion [Proverbs 31] as a picture of the happy housewife would probably not endorse the lifestyle of this woman if they met her on the street. In her ancient Middle Eastern society, she was an entrepreneur. She stayed occupied with her home-based business day and night—and someone else probably watched her children when she was selling linen in the marketplace, dealing with merchants, buying fields, or making wine with the fruit of her vineyard. She was most definitely not a stay-at-home mom in the suburban American sense of the word. Those who use this passage to keep women locked into an exclusively domestic role are mis-using Scripture to hold women in a crippling form of religious bondage.[1]

Women in the workplace also face battles between their own spiritual convictions and the lack of those same values in their coworkers. Diane paid a great price to stand for righteousness and integrity in the workplace. While working as a comptroller for a large corporation, she made a startling discovery: Someone had made entries in the company's financial journals without her knowledge.

After discovering the falsified entries, Diane attempted to correct them, but upper management put pressure on her to "cook the books" by changing her records. Apparently, management wanted the entries to reflect figures that would show they had met the 30 percent compound earnings growth guidance that they had previously reported to the Wall Street analysts, even though they had not. Meeting such guidance generally kept the stock price high and allowed the company's executives to realize significant additional compensation from the sale of stock options.

Diane refused to cooperate in the scheme and was promptly fired. The financial officer informed her that she was being let go because she was not a team player. Someone even stood over her, watching her every move, while she emptied her desk. Diane was devastated, but she did not waver in her commitment to uphold righteous standards at work, regardless of the personal price she had to pay.

Some time later, Diane's former supervisor came to her with tears in his eyes and said that he hoped his changed life would bring her comfort. He explained that when he came to the company, he was, at best, a nominal Christian. He did not even think that he would have gone to heaven if he had died prior to meeting Diane. However, after watching how Diane lived and conducted herself at work, he made a decision to receive the Lord. Later, when Diane needed employment during a time when there were few opportunities, this man (who was by then a vice president and general manager) gave a recommendation that resulted in her getting a position. Diane declares, "God provides supernatural grace and strength to confront unrighteousness in the marketplace, rather than compromising with it just to keep your job, even when you're standing alone."

Diane is just one of many women who face difficulties in the workplace. Other women also struggle with difficult situations, such as not receiving a promotion that is deserved, sexual harassment by coworkers, or being treated differently based solely on their gender. Women in the workplace are discovering that only the Lord can change their situations. Many are forming prayer groups to help change the spiritual environment in their places of employment.

Ruth has seen the power of prayer prosper her company and also bring reward into her own life. She understands that the Lord desires to bless her so that she can be a blessing to others. After joining her company, Ruth quickly became aware of some of the sinful practices in the company's past. So Ruth met with her Marketplace Prayer Warriors group and, similar to Daniel who repented for the sins of Israel's past, stood in a place of repentance for the sins of the company. She repented for unfair business practices, the sin of placing profits ahead of customer welfare, and poor customer support. As she prayed this prayer of identificational repentance for the company, change began to occur.

Ruth knew that the Lord had heard her prayers and that His desire was to begin to bless the company, so she then began to pray for increase. She asked the Lord to bring business from the north, south, east and west. She offered prayers for the Lord to be glorified in all of the company's business dealings.

Slowly but surely, doors of opportunity opened. Not only was the company blessed, but Ruth was blessed as well. As a result of large sales and God's faithfulness in securing several contracts, Ruth won the Sales Rep and Deal of the Year Award for her company. The Lord used Ruth to not only bless her company but also to cause her company to be a blessing to its customers.

Women today are being delivered from the old mind-set that believes that the presence of the Lord is confined to church buildings. These women understand that the church building is the place of equipping for Christians (see Eph. 4:11-12) and that the real ministry is found outside church buildings, often in the workplace. They recognize that Christians are called to be the Lord's image-bearers wherever they go—to reflect the character and power of Jesus in the workplace, in their homes, and anywhere else the Lord sends them.

My husband, Dale, is an engineer and manager for a manufacturing plant. A few years ago, Hahn, a woman supervisor in the plant, came to salvation and was healed of a tumor as a result of Dale's prayers and witness to her. After word spread throughout the plant about Hahn's healing, others came to her and asked her to pray for their healing. Today, Hahn is being used by the Lord as a missionary in the marketplace. She prays with workers who are in distress, angry or upset and those who are in need of the healing power of Jesus. In fact, some of the people in the plant lovingly call her "Doctor." Of course, Hahn always lets them know she is not a doctor, and she then tells them about the Great Physician, Jesus Christ, who can heal their bodies, bring peace to their minds, and give them eternal life.[2]

> *God* is sending women into the workplace for Kingdom purposes. The call to the workplace for women is a high call from the Lord.

God is sending women into the workplace for Kingdom purposes. These women understand they are able and meant to do more than simply perform a job to bring in finances. They are extending God's kingdom. The call to the workplace for women is a high call from the Lord.

Women today are at a watershed moment as they break out of traditional mind-sets and religious bondage. They are embracing new mind-sets and allowing the Lord to rewrite their lives. They are creating lifestyles that bring their passions and values to the forefront. As they forge these new frontiers in the workplace, they are helping to reinvent a living, vital Christianity that changes society.

Of course, discovering these new frontiers for fulfilling God's purpose for your life can happen faster if you have a mentor. But what are some of the characteristics of a good mentor? Is there such a thing as a "toxic mentor"? If so, how can you identify and avoid one? In the next chapter, we will examine some of these aspects of mentoring.

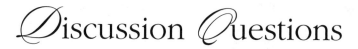 Discussion Questions

1. Discuss the teachings you have received concerning a woman's place in the home.

2. Discuss the teachings you have received concerning women in the workplace.

3. Is there a conflict between God's call for women to the home and God's call for women to the workplace? Have you personally experienced that conflict? If so, how did you resolve it?

4. What are some of the ways a woman in the workplace can extend God's kingdom?

5. How can prayer make a difference for those called to the workplace?

6. Discuss the way support groups can help you fulfill your call to the workplace.

7. Share at least one way the Lord has used you to reflect His presence in your place of employment.

Notes

1. J. Lee Grady, *10 Lies the Church Tells Women* (Lake Mary, FL: Creation House, 2000), p. 157.
2. Barbara Wentroble, *You Are Anointed* (Ventura, CA: Regal Books, 2001), pp. 97-98.

Finding Mentors

Jane is in her thirties and recently started her own business making and selling jewelry. This has been her dream for many years, but now she realizes that the dream was much larger in scope than she originally envisioned. Not only does Jane want to develop her business locally, but she would also like to see it grow and expand to other cities. She realizes, however, that she needs someone to help her reach the potential that the Lord has for her.

Lisa was involved in ministry for about 30 years. She and her husband pastored a church, where she led youth meetings and did a fair amount of traveling and speaking. Because of all the experience she had under her belt, Lisa was asked to mentor other ministers and youth leaders. The request, although encouraging, was at the same time a little overwhelming. It was one thing to be involved in ministry, but something else entirely to be asked to mentor others and help them reach their ministry potential. As Lisa questioned her ability to mentor others, she realized that she needed a mentor of her own—someone who could help her reach the next level. But how would she find such a person?

Jane and Lisa are no different from many other women. Reaching the next level in ministry or business requires change, skills and character development. It also requires forming meaningful relationships with others to help fill the void left by making that change and to help make the transition from one level to the next. The dilemma faced by Jane and Lisa speaks of the individualism in our society that has, to a large degree, become a liability rather than an asset.

Over the years, countless women facing the same predicament have come to me to ask my advice. "You have been my mentor for years," one young lady announced. I looked at her in amazement, stunned that she would consider me her mentor when I had no idea who she was. How could I have been her mentor? Had we met somewhere in the past? Her face was not even familiar to me. If I had served as her mentor, shouldn't I be aware of it?

Since then, I've had similar experiences in which people have come to me after I finished speaking and told me that I have been a mentor to them. It took me a while to understand what they were saying, because I'd always considered a mentor to be someone who was in close contact to the one being mentored. Although that is usually true, I have since learned that not all mentors have a close, personal relationship with the people they influence.

Although there has always been a need for mentors, it is only natural that the need would increase as women are called into leadership. Few people arrive at their destiny alone. Nearly all of us in leadership positions can point to someone who helped us get there. Throughout the generations, people have recognized the need and value of mentoring. Fathers mentored sons and mothers mentored daughters. Jesus was the supreme example of a mentor: He spent more time training a few people to change the course of history than He did in preparing a sermon to dazzle the crowds.

Many families today are what we would term "dysfunctional." Often, the parents in these families are too busy building their own careers, or they simply do not understand the responsibility of how to prepare children to achieve their destinies. Other families are broken and unable to get past their own hurts. Churches sometimes suffer the same malady. Pastors can get so caught up in building their own ministry that they fail to understand the responsibility of raising up the next generation.

I can think of a number of people who have encouraged and helped me through the years. Yet, to say that I had a mentor would be stretching the truth. Most groups and individuals with whom I was in contact were struggling to build their own ministries. I was simply a helper to get them where they were going.

Because I was so hungry for all the Lord had for me, I read every Christian book I could find, attended seminars and conferences, devoured the Bible and Bible study books, and spent a lot of time seeking the Lord in prayer. As a result, the Lord enabled me to get to where I am today, though I know that I have not yet arrived at the place He is taking me. Looking back, I believe the path I took was not the best one. If I'd had a mentor, I could have reached the place I am today faster and with fewer detours.

Today, I want others to go farther than I have gone and reach their destinies more quickly than I reached mine. I want them to avoid some of the obstacles that hindered me along the way. As a result, I have dedicated my life to making that happen. With God's grace, I, along with many other mentors, will have the privilege of unlocking the treasures within future generations. We can never find our own fulfillment if we focus solely on fulfilling our own God-given destinies; we must also seek to help others fulfill theirs! I love the way author Fred Smith described a mentor with this same type of heart: "A mentor is not a person who can do the work better than his followers; he is a person who can get his followers to do the work better than he can."[1]

The term "mentoring," sometimes referred to as "coaching," is simply the process of helping someone develop unique qualities in the art of learning. Mentoring is really about character development. Character is best developed through the assistance of a mentor or coach who is able to see the potential beyond a person's weaknesses.

Maria Woodworth-Etter was the recipient of excellent mentoring at the age of 13 from a preacher who saw her potential. This preacher led Maria to the Lord at the beginning of the Third Great Awakening (a period of revival in America from 1858 to 1908) and prayed that her life would be a shining light. I am sure that this preacher never realized that Maria would become the grandmother of the Pentecostal Movement and that her influence would spread throughout the world. Yet, he must have sensed the hand of the Lord on Maria's life and God's great potential inside her. His affirmation was enough to release the potential that God had placed within her.

> *Mentoring is simply the process of helping someone develop unique qualities in the art of learning.*

I read somewhere that the greatest athletes usually come from small schools and that it takes a scout to find those individuals and identify the potential in them. All of us need someone to help us get to where we are willing to go. Similar to an athletic scout, a mentor is not someone who is trying to make someone else perfect. The goal is improvement, not perfection. Mentors bring improvement into our lives because they see the potential that we often can't see in ourselves.

There is an adage among old-time Pentecostal women that goes something like this: "If you have it, you will get there. If you don't have it, you won't." What this suggests is that we don't need anyone's help to reach or fulfill our destinies—we either have God's call on our life or we don't. How very untrue this old adage is, and how sad that many women have similar beliefs!

Women have struggled for years to get where God wants to take them, encountering tremendous obstacles along the way. Yet many have just given up and decided that God didn't have anything for them, since they themselves didn't seem to have it. But women no longer have to buy in to this faulty thinking. Today, God is raising up true mentors who will see the potential in women and stand with them as they pursue God's call on their lives.

There are certain qualities that you should keep in mind when seeking a mentor. First, a good mentor should share your philosophy of life. The Bible says, "Can two walk together, unless they are agreed?" (Amos 3:3, *NKJV*). The obvious answer is no. How can two people walk together if they are headed in different directions?

One of the ways to be sure that you and your potential mentor are headed in the same direction is by asking yourself if you view this person as a worthy and reputable role model. In other words, you should be able to look at your potential mentor and see something that you would want in your own life, a "deposit" of God that you are willing to exert whatever effort is necessary to obtain for yourself. A good mentor will be more than willing to walk with you until that deposit of God is released within you.

Elisha recognized a deposit of God in Elijah. He refused to stop following after his role model until he received the same measure of anointing from God in his own life. Wherever Elijah went, Elisha was faithful to follow. As a result of the faithfulness of Elisha to his mentor, Elisha received a double portion of the anointing that was upon Elijah (see 2 Kings 2:1-14). The payoff for following Elijah was well worth the price.

The second quality or characteristic of a good mentor is that he or she will guide you as a protégé, tugging on your potential to see it released. Because the "pulling" will often be uncomfortable for you and may even produce insecurity within you, this process will require great endurance on your part. I am known by many for the way that I pull on the potential inside those around me. I do so because I see the destiny locked inside them and am determined to do whatever I can to unlock that destiny.

Falma Rufus is one such individual in whom I saw potential and pulled until it was released. Falma is an incredible woman of God who leads the intercessors for my ministry and ministers all around the world. One of the reasons her ministry is so loved and welcomed is because she sings the song of the Lord in a very powerful way. But it wasn't always like this.

Several years ago, I was speaking at an out-of-town meeting. Falma and several of our intercessors surprised me by coming to this conference to pray for me, but I knew that God wanted something more from their visit. During one of the sessions, I asked Falma to come to the platform. I then whispered in her ear, "I am going to prophesy over several people. When I do, I want you to sing the song of the Lord over them." Falma's eyes became as big as saucers! She had never done that before. Noticing her reaction, I again whispered in Falma's ear, "I know this is going to stretch you, but it will be good for you."

As I called each person forward, I spoke what I sensed the Lord was saying to each individual. As I finished speaking over each person, Falma opened her mouth and sang the most beautiful and encouraging song from the Lord, and the musicians accompanied her as if they had rehearsed all afternoon. The atmosphere was electric with the presence of the Lord!

Later, the worship leader told us that he thought we ministered that way all the time. He was shocked to discover that this was the first time it had happened! But even though it was the first time, it certainly wasn't the last. Not only does Falma now sing like this on a regular basis but many of our intercessors now also do the same thing. God not only unlocked the potential in Falma, but He also used her to unlock the potential in an entire company of prophetic intercessors!

The forces of darkness tried for years to keep Falma from reaching her destiny. She and her husband, who was frequently abusive to her, lived in the inner city in a culture that encouraged women to live in subservience to men. Falma's husband was a policeman and an ordained minister, but he did not honor or esteem his wife as the Bible commanded him to do. Eventually, he came to the saving knowledge of Jesus and passed on to be with Him in heaven.

With the power of God in Falma's life, she now lives in the freedom of the Lord and has founded a ministry called "Pray His Song." Falma is also a chaplain at the Dallas County Juvenile Detention Center, where she brings hope to troubled young girls. Her ministry is power-packed, not only in the city where she resides, but also in other regions and nations.

The third quality or characteristic of good mentors is that they have a tolerance for mistakes. When our oldest son, Brian, was about 14 months old, we decided that it was time for him to walk without holding on to sofas or chairs. He had grown accustomed to the security of holding on to furniture as he carefully walked around the room, but he needed to learn to let go and move out on his own. As Dale and I sat facing each other on the floor, we stood Brian between us. "Come on, Brian," I called to him. "Walk to Mommy. You can do it! You're a big boy. You can walk. Come on."

Brian took a few steps and then fell. We picked him up, stood him on his feet, and applauded his efforts: "Yay, Brian! You did well. You walked a long way." Then we started again. "Come on. You can do it. Walk to Daddy this time." Even though Brian's little wobbly legs let him fall a few times, he continued to make progress. Within three days, he wasn't just walking—he was running!

Rather than pointing out the number of times Brian fell, we cheered him on each time he made a little progress. In the same way, a good mentor will reward your progress with affirming words rather than focusing on or being intolerant of your mistakes. It is one thing to correct someone's course, but another thing to demand perfection. Even correction should be done in a loving spirit that encourages improvement. None of us are perfect, but we should all be working to improve.

A fourth characteristic of good mentors is that they will have a vision for the future and be able to point out to those they mentor practical steps on how to achieve that vision. All of us have blind spots in our lives—things we simply cannot see. Our mentors need to be able to see where the Lord is taking us. Sometimes, all it takes to get us moving in the right direction is the suggestion of some practical steps from someone whom we respect and know has our best interests at heart.

Patty called me one day to express her disappointments over some things she had failed to do in the past, one of which was never going to college. When I asked her if she still wanted to do that, she replied, "Today, I would rather go to Bible school instead of college." Patty's response helped me to identify the next step she needed to take. I recommended that she look at correspondence courses or schools close to her home. "Begin to do what you would like to do with your life," I told her. Today, Patty is enrolled in a Bible school so that she can fulfill a dream that is in her heart. She simply needed someone to encourage her to fulfill her vision, rather than allow her to continue to spend years in regret.

You may not be able to find the perfect mentor, but you should be able to find a person who can impart to you the qualities and skills you need.

The final characteristic or quality of good mentors is that they possess the particular gifts and abilities necessary to build up and encourage others. You may not be able to find the perfect, ideal mentor. However, you should be able to find a person who can impart to you the qualities and skills you need. Keep in mind that your goals may require more than one mentor, and allow the Lord to connect you with various mentors throughout your life. I guarantee that you will be richer and more fulfilled as a result.

Just as good mentors can be identified by certain qualities and characteristics, bad mentors can be identified by what I consider "toxic" characteristics. One of these characteristics is the mentor's lack of availability when you are in the greatest need. It is true that you will need to learn how to handle difficult situations, but times of crisis will inevitably arise when you will need someone whom you know will be there to understand and counsel you. One of the things I say to those I mentor is, "If I can't be there for you when you need help, what good am I?" Find someone who will teach you how to lean on the Lord and seek His counsel but who also will not desert you in times of great need.

Another characteristic of a toxic mentor is one who is overly critical and controlling. Cynthia and her husband, who were pastoring a church, were the parents of a chronically ill child. At the time, Cynthia was feeling lonely, isolated and insecure. She was not intentionally looking for a mentor, but she knew that she needed help to advance in God. Cynthia came under a toxic mentor during this time of tenuous emotional instability. The mentor had once been a speaker at their church, and the two had become friends. Cynthia describes the relationship this way:

> Over time, I noticed that this person spoke ill of everyone she had ministered with, both in the past and in current relationships. Whenever I shared a revelation or insight with her, she minimized it, dismissed it or implied that it originated with her. She discounted my gifts if they seemed to be on a par with hers. She also placed herself between me and God, in the sense that she would decide if God had spoken something to me or not.
>
> Over a period of time, I lost confidence in myself. Our church lost deacons, most of our intercessors, and many others as a result of her influence. The church ultimately ended in a split. Worst of all, my relationship with this person created a deep division between me and my husband.
>
> I now have a covenant relationship with a good mentor, and I am able to value myself as well as others. This time around, I spent time searching for a God-ordained mentor, and I am so thankful that I found one. My cur-

rent mentoring relationship is based on mutual trust, respect and accountability. I believe that I have almost fully recovered from this experience and am now back on track with my destiny.

Many potential Falmas, Maria Woodworth-Etters, Pattys and Cynthias cry out to the Lord for a mentor. They are looking for true mentors who will model the life of Jesus to them. They cry out for deliverance and healing from the devastation of toxic mentors, yet they continue their quest to be connected to mentors who will come alongside them to help them reach their destiny. Terese Holloway recently sent me a poem she wrote that carries the cry from the hearts of these women today:

When you climb the hill before me,
    will you tell me what you see?
For each victory *you* accomplish
    will most surely speak to me.
You see, my climb is often gruesome,
    and I sometimes feel I'll fall;
So I need someone who's been there
    and kept their focus upon God.

Your words to cheer me on
    will really help me in my climb;
I'm convinced they'll spur me on
    until I reach the finish line.
So, please don't leave me hanging
    upon the mountain wall,
For the guidance that *you* offer
    just might keep *me* from a fall.

All it takes is but a moment
    to encourage me in my despair;
To let me know *you* made it through
    every obstacle and snare.
Yes, my heart will be so grateful
    if you will stop and take the time
To help *me* scale the mountain
    by merely letting *your* light shine.

Remember, not every mentor is right for you. Trust God to help you find the person who will help you do what He has designed, equipped and called you to do.

Now that you understand the importance of getting connected to a mentor, you are ready to have the greatness on the inside of you released. What does that greatness look like? What did God put inside of you that is now ready to come forth and bless the earth? In the next chapter, we will look at your God-given potential and the incredible possibilities that await you in the days ahead.

Discussion Questions

1. Define the word "mentor" in your own words.

2. Name and describe at least three qualities that you are looking for in a mentor.

3. Describe at least two characteristics of toxic mentors.

4. Write about some painful experiences you have had with toxic mentors.

5. Write about your experiences with a good mentor.

6. How would you counsel someone looking for a mentor?

7. What is the main thing you have taken away from a positive mentoring relationship?

Note
1. Fred Smith, quoted in Ted W. Engstrom, *The Fine Art of Mentoring* (Brentwood, TN: Wolgemuth and Hyatt, Publishers, Inc.), p. 13.

Chosen for Greatness

I was standing in church during a worship service several years ago when Fran, the woman next to me, quietly whispered in my ear, "I am going into the hospital this week to have a mastectomy. The doctor has diagnosed me with cancer. He feels my condition is very serious."

My first thought was that I should encourage her to go to the altar at the end of the service and have the elders pray for her. My next thought was that I should pray for her right away, but I didn't want to do anything to interrupt the worship service. So I stood there, wrestling with my thoughts. I wanted to do everything decently and in the order the Bible prescribes, but I also sensed that God wanted me to pray for that lady then and there.

Finally, I leaned over and prayed quietly in Fran's ear, "Father, this is Your child. She is in covenant with You. Jesus paid the price for her healing. Healing is her birthright as a child of God. You have given me the authority as your daughter to take dominion over all the attacks of the enemy. I command this cancer to leave this body. I command every abnormal cell to leave her body. I release the healing power of Jesus to flow into her body from head to toe. In the name of Jesus, be healed!"

About 20 minutes later, Fran had to leave. She had an appointment and was unable to stay until the end of the service to receive prayer from the elders. How thankful I was that I had prayed for her while she was there!

On Tuesday morning, my phone rang. It was Fran, calling me from the hospital. When the doctors performed the surgery, they could not find any cancer in her body. Jesus had healed her!

> God takes ordinary people like you and me and puts His extraordinary nature inside us.

Although the doctors did several follow-up procedures, they were never able to find the cancer that had been documented on medical records prior to the surgery.

Years have passed since that occasion, and I have since experienced God's miracle-working power numerous times. However, praying for and releasing God's healing power is not a special gift for a few spiritual "superstars"; it is the inheritance of every believer (see Mark 16:16-18). Although the former generations in your family may not have received their inheritance, you can break that old generational cycle. Your family may not have followed the Lord; they may not have been aware of God's power that was available to them. Whatever the reason, you do not have to be denied what the Lord has planned for your life. Greatness is on the inside of you, just waiting to be released.

God takes ordinary people like you and me and puts His extraordinary nature inside us. God planned this for your life before you were even born. In fact, God's plan for your life came about before He flung the stars into the sky and long before there was a clock or calendar to mark time. God planned for your life before He set galaxies on their course or before He created the earth and set the sun and moon in place. "Blessed be the God and Father of our Lord Jesus Christ, who has blessed us with every spiritual blessing in the heavenly places in Christ, *just as He chose us in Him before the foundation of the world*, that we should be holy and blameless before Him" (Eph. 1:3-4, emphasis added).

I like to think of God creating His plan for our lives at a board of directors meeting in heaven before time ever began. God the Father, God the Son, and God the Holy Spirit met together to plan your very life and destiny. You were in the heart of God before you were ever in the thoughts of your parents. You were in the heart of God before anything was created. You are not an accident or a mistake—you are part of the perfect and divine plan of God! As such, greatness resides within you and is waiting to be released. You, like Queen Esther, were born for such a time as this (see Esther 4:14). So why is this concept so difficult for some women to accept? Some reasons include:

- They feel that they were born at an inopportune time.
- They believe that their birth caused or added to their parents' financial difficulties.
- They were born to parents who had a strained relationship with each other.
- They were born out of wedlock.
- They came into a family in which there were already many children, and their parents did not want another child.

This list is certainly not complete and could easily include many other situations. But regardless of the circumstances surrounding your birth, you need to remember that only God is the giver of life. The circumstances surrounding your birth may have seemed all wrong, but it was God who determined the time and place of your birth. He brought you into the world to fulfill His destiny today. "For thou didst form my inward parts: Thou didst cover me in my mother's womb" (Ps. 139:13, *ASV*).

Dr. Cheryl Green could have used the excuse that she came into the world at the wrong time and that the circumstances of her birth excluded her from any greatness in her life. Cheryl is African-American, disabled, and grew up in a family that more often than not was homeless. She was born with a rare condition called arthrogryposis multiplex congenital, which left her with undeveloped lower limbs (or "a mangled mess," as she describes it). She survived many painful, life-threatening surgeries and endured continual abuse from her mentally ill parents.

In high school, while other girls were talking about the prom, Cheryl and her family were living in their car. Before classes began in the morning, Cheryl would wash and change her clothes in the school bathroom. Yet she did not allow these circumstances to stop her from achieving greatness in her life. She went on to win an academic scholarship to Yale University. She also filed and won a lawsuit against Yale, because the facilities at the school were not handicap-friendly.

Cheryl now has a doctorate from Southern Methodist University in Dallas and serves as a dean at Eastfield College. She has authored two books, including *Child of Promise: One Woman's Journey from Tragedy to Triumph,* in which she chronicles her story of overcoming horrendous challenges. Cheryl overcame extreme poverty, disability, and a dysfunctional family by making a decision to allow the greatness of God to be released in her life so that she could fulfill her destiny as God's woman.

It is the greatness of God in each of us that helps us secure the victory for every situation we face. But what does this greatness look like? How do we recognize or identify it?

First, God's greatness gives us the ability to overcome great obstacles and challenges. The book of Revelation gives many promises of reward to those who overcome. Again, Cheryl is a wonderful example. To step into her destiny, she had to overcome obstacles of poverty, a dysfunctional family, and physical disability.

A second picture of God's greatness is His healing power, which is available for every believer. I have seen the Lord heal countless people through the years, including those with cancer, broken bones, heart conditions, hopeless blood disorders, and many other life-threatening conditions. Of course, God's healing power is not just for physical conditions—many times over the years, I have seen God heal broken hearts and unstable minds. It is His desire to flow His healing power through you to heal the wounded hearts and emotions of others. God's healing power is not just for a chosen few; it belongs to every child of God, including you!

I love what Fr. Gaynor Banks says about the true center of our being, where the Lord abides and is released in us:

> There is a Center in every man in which and through which God works. To that Center He speaks; through that Center He acts. When a man discovers his own divine Center, he stands at the gateway to powerful living.[1]

Life must be lived out of this Center in us that houses the presence of the Lord. When we live out of this Center, we find that the power of God's greatness overcomes every adversity and every circumstance designed to block our destiny as women of God.

The circumstances of our lives as women do not always happen the way we had hoped. Many of the women in the Bible had difficult circumstances to overcome. One of my favorite examples is a relatively unknown woman by the name of Rizpah. Although her story is tucked away in a few verses of the Old Testament, it is one that can bring hope to all women.

Rizpah lived in the face of devastating loss in almost every area of her life. She was born into a family of poverty and was given a name that means "pavement." Pavement is something to be walked on, and throughout Rizpah's life, she lived up to her name. She was walked on by her circumstances, and yet she was still able to rise above her situation because of her great faith and her intercession. Through this greatness of God inside of her, Rizpah overcame the lowly position of being King Saul's concubine, rather than his wife (see 2 Sam. 3:7). She overcame the loss of her sons, and she used her intercession to strengthen her until rain fell from heaven (see 2 Sam. 21:8-10).

Glenda Malmin, in her book about the life of Rizpah titled *The Hidden Power of Undefeatable Faith,* offers the following hope to women who are facing adverse circumstances:

Breakthrough is born in the womb of adversity. Undefeatable faith is born in the womb of adversity. Expect a miracle of healing for your wounded heart or your misguided perspective on your personal value . . . *today.* It's on the way; the miracle is in the womb of your heart. Stay close to the Word of God and to the Presence of God, for the miracle is very near. Remember that God's Word says you are His child, His creation, well planned and greatly loved. He thinks about you, He loves you, He enjoys you, He designed you for a specific reason, and you are a blessing to Him just as you are.[2]

Women called to the ministry often find that life does not always happen the way they had envisioned it. Kathryn Kuhlman was a powerful woman who saw thousands of people healed in her meetings, yet she ended up marrying a man whom she had been warned about. Immediately after the wedding, Kathryn left her new husband and went to see a friend, weeping and admitting that the marriage had been a mistake. Some people have said that what made Kathryn great was her choice to recover from her mistake. The way she dealt with her own mistakes produced the powerful revelation behind her sermons on temptation, forgiveness and victory.

It is not necessary to have a worldwide ministry, be a CEO of a corporation or become a government leader in order to release God's potential inside us.

> *We* should never minimize the importance of the way the Lord made us. He put His nature in us so that others could see His greatness.

Sometimes we are looking for big things in our life when God sees what we would call little things. God says that when we are faithful in the small things, He will give us more. These little or seemingly insignificant abilities in our lives are the result of God's greatness being manifested through us. We should never minimize the importance of the way the Lord made us. He put His nature in us so that others could see His greatness.

As a young child, Ruth did not understand that God had destined her for great things. When she was 11 years old, a coach saw her swimming at a YMCA. This man had been a coach for several Olympic swimmers, and he decided to approach Ruth's

parents to get permission to train her. Since her family had limited resources, he offered to train her for free. Both Ruth and her
parents were flattered and gladly accepted his proposal.

Greatness usually requires sacrifice in order to reach the potential God has for us, but Ruth didn't know that when she excitedly
began her training. She soon learned that achieving greatness
would cost her more than she could ever have dreamed. Her gruel-
ing training began at 6 A.M. with a routine that included working
out with weights and pulleys and running laps. Several more hours
of workouts awaited her at the end of the school day. It was an all-
consuming schedule that affected not only Ruth but her parents
and siblings as well, as Ruth's mother became the facilitator to
enable her daughter to participate in the training events.

Ruth followed this schedule for two years until she contracted pneumonia three times one winter. Her lungs were seriously
damaged, and she was forced to make a decision, due to her health
situation, not to continue to pursue her goal. But God in His wisdom had a plan for Ruth's life. Even though it looked as if she had
missed the purpose for her life, all was not lost. As a result of her
training as a swimmer, she was able to pay her way through college by working as a lifeguard. She coached the swim team and
water ballet teams and gave individual swimming lessons for the
Red Cross.

Ruth now realizes that God put greatness inside of her because
His plan for her was to succeed. He made a way for her to rise above
limited finances, poor health and other limitations to become the
woman of God that she is today. Her education, which she was able
to finance because of her swimming ability, has enabled her to
position herself in a high place in the corporate world. It is easy to
see in her words that she gives the Lord all the credit and honor for
what He has done in her life:

While the Lord did not direct me to the Olympics, I did experience the cost and rewards of being the best. When the coach noticed my swimming talents, he saw greatness in me that no one else had noticed. His investment of time and resources encouraged me to be the best. I believe that the Lord has used this situation to help me strive for greatness for His kingdom.

As believers, we have God's greatness on the inside. This greatness will help us run the race of life so that we may finish well, just as the apostle Paul testified of himself in the book of Acts: "But I do not consider my life of any account as dear to myself, so that I may finish my course and the ministry which I received from the Lord Jesus, to testify solemnly of the gospel of the grace of God" (Acts 20:24).

Although there is a price to pay in order to obtain the rewards of God's greatness, the rewards are well worth the cost. At the end of our race as women, may we be able to say with those who have gone before us, "I have fought the good fight, I have finished the course, I have kept the faith" (2 Tim. 4:7).

*D*iscussion *Q*uestions

1. What are some of the unexpected situations that you have faced?

2. How did you handle these situations?

3. Is there anything that you would do differently now than when the situation occurred?

4. Describe what you sense greatness looks like in the life of a Christian.

5. How do you release the greatness of God in your life?

6. What would you like to be said of you at the end of your race?

Notes

1. Fr. Gaynor Banks, quoted in Leanne Payne, *The Healing Presence* (Westchester, IL: Crossway Books, 1989), p. 71.
2. Glenda Malmin, *The Hidden Power of Undefeatable Faith* (Portland, OR: City Bible Publishing, 2004), p. 156.

A Hope and a Future

As I was growing up, I never even so much as imagined myself doing what I am doing today! Traveling throughout the nations to call women to arise and break out of old mind-sets was definitely not on my agenda. I saw myself as a timid, quiet person, living what I considered a normal, mundane life. You may be able to relate in some way to my old way of thinking.

Today, the Lord is issuing a clarion call to women trapped in similar mind-sets. I have good news for you: God planned your life and your future before time began. God is the giver of life, and He knew exactly the purpose that He had ordained for you. It was in the fullness of time that He brought you into this world, and now He desires you to shift into His ordained destiny.

As you make this shift into the new place that God has created for you, it is important that you grab hold of your future. If you have received a prophetic promise from the Lord, hold on to it regardless of how long it takes to come to pass. Prophecy is not automatically fulfilled; it requires action on the part of the one to whom the prophecy is given. Prophetic promise, therefore, is conditional. You have a responsibility to allow the prophetic word to come to pass, which means you need to do something. You need to pray, obey the things God asks you to do, and stand in faith for the promise to manifest in your life.

The prophet Jeremiah discovered this when God spoke a prophetic promise to him at a time in which there seemed to be nothing but destruction in sight. "'For I know the plans that I have for you,' declares the Lord, 'plans to prosper you and not to harm you, plans to give you hope and a future'" (Jer. 29:11, *NIV*). That prophetic word came at a time when Jeremiah's people were about to be taken into captivity. Life must have looked very dark at that point, with little reason to hope for a good future ahead. Yet the Lord knew what Jeremiah did not know: The prophet would finish and fulfill the destiny God had planned for him.

God knows the same thing about you. It doesn't matter where you are today or where you have been in the past. God has a hope and a future for you, and because of that, you are able to finish and fulfill the destiny God planned for you since before the beginning of time.

Many people start well, but they don't finish well. Recently, I was reminiscing about some people I knew many years ago. They were the spiritual giants in our city when I first came into my walk with the Lord. Today, their lives are filled with broken relationships, broken dreams and broken hope. Somewhere along the path of life, they made some turns that led them away from God's destiny for them. Now they are quick to blame others for their place in life, rather than repenting and accepting responsibility for their own actions so that they can be restored to the path and destiny God has for them.

I learned a long time ago that my problem is not other people or my circumstances in life. I agree with the old saying, "I have found the problem, and it is me." Only I can lean on the Lord and go where He is taking me. It is my responsibility to let Him enlarge my vision. I must wake up each day and receive fresh hope from the Lord. Others can encourage me. They can see the potential in me. They can prophesy God's promise to me. They can do a lot of things to help me along life's journey. But, the one thing they cannot do is position me into my destiny. Only I, with the help of the Lord, can do that. I am responsible for finishing well in life, and more than anything else, I want to do that. I am sure you feel the same way.

Could it be possible that you and I can break out of the old religious, traditional and emotional mind-sets that have kept generations of women from their destinies in life? Is it possible that you and I can lead future generations of women into all that Jesus accomplished for them through His death on the cross? Do you think that you and I can finish well the race that is set before us?

What if God called you to go to a nation like Iraq or Afghanistan? What if you went to those nations and became part of those countries' transformation? What if you were called to be a judge and bring justice to your area? What if you were called to serve on the local school board and make critical changes in your school system? What if you were called to be a stay-at-home mom and raise godly, law-abiding children?

Each of us is called to be a significant person who can make a difference in our world. Corrie ten Boom was simply a daughter of a clock and watch shop owner during the Nazi invasion of the Netherlands, but she and her family provided protection for hundreds of Jews. As a result, they were arrested and sent to concentration camps. Although others in her family died in the camps, Corrie survived and went on to tell the story of God's faithfulness. Eventually, she traveled the world and authored best-selling books, and her story was turned into the movie

The Hiding Place. Corrie's testimony has touched countless lives.

Though most of us will not become famous like Corrie ten Boom, we all have a significant role in the kingdom of God. How wonderful it will be for us at the end of life's journey if someone says of us, as was said of King David, "[he] served the purpose of God in his own generation" (Acts 13:36).

Other Books by
Barbara Wentroble

Prophetic Intercession
Unlocking Miracles and Releasing the Blessings of God

Praying with Authority
*How to Release the Authority of Heaven So the Will
of God Is Done on Earth*

God's Purpose for Your Life
Getting to Where God Wants You to Be!

You Are Anointed
God Has an Extraordinary Plan for Your Life